A MATTER OF LIFE AND TECHNOLOGY

Health Sciences
Today

A MATTER OF LIFE AND TECHNOLOGY

Health Sciences Today

ESSIE E. LEE Ed.D.

JULIAN MESSNER  NEW YORK
A Division of Simon & Schuster, Inc.

ACKNOWLEDGEMENTS

The publishers and author would like to thank the many people and institutions who generously helped in the preparation of this book by supplying information and photographs. In particular we would like to thank New York Hospital-Cornell Medical Center, Bellevue Hospital, The Mount Sinai Medical Center and Columbia Presbyterian Medical Center for supplying photographs and for helping with the research.

Published by Julian Messner,
A Division of Simon & Schuster, Inc.
Simon & Schuster Building
Rockefeller Center
1230 Avenue of the Americas
New York, New York 10020

10 9 8 7 6 5 4 3 2

JULIAN MESSNER and colophon are
trademarks of Simon & Schuster, Inc.

Manufactured in the United States of America

Library of Congress Cataloging-in-Publication Data

Lee, Essie E.
   A matter of life and technology.

   Includes bibliographies and index.
   1. Medical innovation.   2. Medicine—Research.
I. Title.   [DNLM: 1. Medicine—trends—popular
works.
WB 130 L477m]
R850.L44   1986   610   86-18233
ISBN 0-671-49847-9

Contents

Introduction

Spectacular is a word that describes what's happened in the past ten years in the health sciences—so says Dr. Joseph A. Buda, vascular surgeon at Columbia Presbyterian Medical Center in New York City. As we near the beginning of the twenty-first century, fantastic technological triumphs set the scene for an exciting and challenging period in medical history. Some of these are in the developmental stages: noninvasive products that make it possible to diagnose diseased tissue without performing radical surgery; surgical lasers that remove polyps and other tissues without opening the body; gene probes and man-made antibodies that cure and treat diseased tissue; materials that repair and replace human tissue; microcomputers that can control and maintain patient care; and sensors that can measure internal substances, such as blood chemistry, without entering the body. New drugs and new ways of administering them, new surgical techniques, simpler and more efficient procedures, better designed equipment for rehabilitation and care, and more accurate diagnosis all add up to a brighter prognosis for patients.

Twenty-five years ago, a doctor might have offered a painkiller and advised the patient to go home and make the best of a bad situation. Some diagnoses meant certain death. Others had a low rate of recovery. Congenital disabilities, as well as disabilities resulting from injuries, meant a limited life style and life span for millions of people. Tiny, premature babies had little chance of survival. Doctors and medical scientists searched for answers but were often handicapped by traditional knowledge and technology. Now all of this is changing because of private and government agencies' interest and support.

The National Institutes of Health—a $5.5 billion agency of the United States Department of Health and Human Services—is the world's foremost biomedical research facility. The agency supports more than 20,000 research projects every year at medical schools across the country. And that's in addition to the work carried out at its Bethesda, Maryland, headquarters.

Kidney transplantation—a dramatic procedure twenty years ago—is now almost routine. Antirejection drugs eventually will make heart and lung transplants quite common, too. As the bank of "spare parts" grows, people in the future can expect to replace vital organs, joints, skin, hair, and parts of the eye. With advances in plastic surgery, we may have a "bionic man or woman" whose normal life span could be 115 years!

Emergency medical procedures from the aerospace industry are not only saving lives but reducing complications and crippling. Microsurgery is saving hands and feet to perform normally again.

Computers permit health practitioners to peer harmlessly into places they never could see before, and they observe processes that were impossible to reach—much less watch. Besides computers, there are robots, bloodless surgery with intense laser beams, implants, and microscopes that can magnify and examine the surface and internal structures of living cells.

New video and telecommunications make it possible to communicate with the aid of computers through telephone lines, special cables, and satellites. There are "smart" wheelchairs, talking thermometers, cash registers and scales, machines that read books, and devices that help the deaf to hear.

But the most revolutionary idea of all comes from scientists at the Los Alamos National Laboratory in New Mexico. They have created the "research rat" of the future. It is the computer program that duplicates the complex system of the human body. This "rat" is a living computer data bank that gives access to ten million pieces of information on what happens when any chemically recognized substance is taken into the body. It will allow researchers in the year 2000 to conduct experiments without using human or animal "guinea pigs."

This book will reveal some of the newest products of research and technology. The "star wars" machines may seem awesome, but they represent future trends in health professionals' commitment to saving lives as well as to improving the quality of life.

Despite the recent fatal *Challenger* launching there will be more launchings in the future. NASA scientists have been studying the disaster and have discovered some possible causes of this tragedy.

The United States space station, scheduled to be operational by the late 1990s, poses many challenges for health care. NASA has contracted the Maryland Institute for Emergency Medical Services to assist in the development of a computerized, miniaturized health care station that will be used in health maintenance and in diagnosing and treating illness and injury during extended missions in space.

One problem is the rescue of personnel who become sick or injured while constructing or manning the space station for three-to-six-month periods. In addition to astronauts, there will be scientists, technicians, observers, and members of the military working in such areas as construction, satellite servicing, material processing, the manufacture of alloys, and scientific research. Construction accidents, the bends, or toxic exposure are some of the problems space station personnel may encounter. NASA has said that it would take twenty-one days to operate a successful rescue mission. How can the injured wait twenty-one days without diagnoses or treatment? These are critical areas for future study by NASA. Meanwhile, some fallout from space medicine is already in use. The first chapter will reveal how some of these outer space miracles are being performed in emergency care right here on earth.

CHAPTER 1

Dial 911

"**M**y baby is not breathing!" "Come quick. A kid just fell out of a window." "My chest hurts. Hurry!" "Help me. I think I'm dying." "Three cars just crashed at the corner." "My baby is coming! I need a doctor." "*Vente! Vente! Tengo mucho dolor.*"

These are just some examples of the frantic calls received every hour of every day by the Emergency Medical Services (EMS) staff. But before help can be sent, certain information has to be entered into the computer. The Call Receiving Operator (CRO) must determine the real nature of the illness and the degree of emergency care needed.

EMERGENCY MEDICAL SERVICES

Most Emergency Medical Services provide Basic Life Support Units with Emergency Medical Technicians (EMTs).

1

For more complicated care, paramedics are available to give Advanced Life Support. These highly trained men and women can do anything short of surgery in the streets to bring back, stabilize, and maintain the life of a seriously ill or injured person. In these situations, every second counts— the earlier that treatment can be administered, the better. And more and more, high technology, including computers, lends support.

The computer verifies the location and gives the call a high or low emergency rating and job number even before the ambulance is dispatched. The time is also recorded. With the aid of a computer, the dispatcher can learn the availability and location of every ambulance within his or her jurisdiction. If needed, the dispatcher can recall a "job in progress" to the screen and add information. The dispatcher can also view additional calls for the same incident or review in the computer a message radioed in by the street crew.

When there is a disaster such as a building cave-in, earthquake, bomb explosion, collapse of a construction crane, multiple car crash, or extensive five-alarm fire, a computer's many functions become vital. The computer ties in with the police department's dispatch system and exchanges information or calls and supplies time estimates of arriving units.

When an ill or injured person is lying in the street waiting for an ambulance, it seems like an eternity. But it usually isn't. In New York City, the average response time for an EMS ambulance answering a top-priority emergency call is 9.4 minutes. This new speed record was announced on September 1, 1985, by Dr. Alexander Kuehl, vice-president of EMS. Dr. Kuehl credited the speedier responses to a

New York City firemen give mouth-to-mouth resusitation to a young victim of smoke inhalation.

substantial increase in personnel and ambulance units. In New York City, there are now 1100 technicians and 270 paramedics using 165 ambulances. Because the ambulances patrol the streets instead of being parked in hospital garages, they reach their destinations more quickly. In addition, the dispatch system is fully computerized and sends health teams out on more than 680,000 calls a year.

The emergency room staff at Bellevue Medical Center, which is designated as a Specialty Care Referral Center, specializes in trauma and the reattachment of limbs. The center is equipped to care for multitraumatized patients—

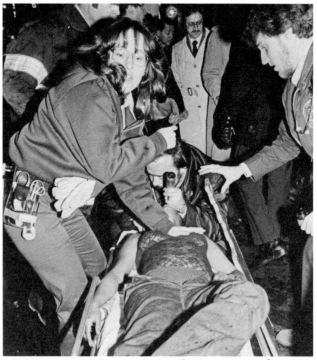

Christine Garafola, an EMS technician, at work on a busy New York street.

victims hurt in fires in the subways, train derailments, airplane crashes, bomb explosions, and building collapses. One of the most publicized catastrophes that ever involved EMS concerned Mrs. Briget Gerney.

A Major Catastrophe

On May 30, 1985, shortly before noon, forty-nine-year-old Briget Gerney was walking along Third Avenue in New York City. She was on her way to lunch when it seemed as if the sky fell on top of her. A fifty-ton crane toppled over, crushing her legs as she lay in a nearly upside-down position pinned just inside the edge of a forty-foot foundation pit. She stayed in this position for about six hours. Rescuers braced fallen machinery with a larger crane brought in from Queens and extricated the injured woman at about 5:55 P.M. Mrs. Gerney remained conscious and talked to her rescuers throughout the long afternoon. Paramedics not only encouraged and cheered her but, at one low point, even gave her the Catholic Church's last rites. The priest was not allowed to get too close to Mrs. Gerney in view of the danger, so the communion host

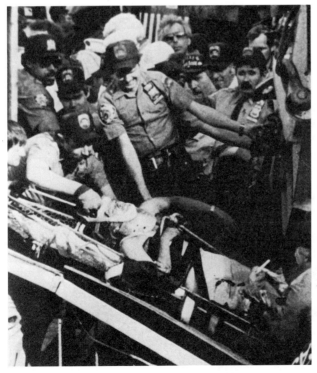

Mrs. Briget Gerney being removed from the below the street pit where she spent six hours. Police and EMS lift her gently from beneath the crane.

was passed from the priest to the brave woman by a paramedic.

When Mrs. Gerney was wheeled into an eleventh-floor operating room at Bellevue Hospital, she became part of medical history. While Dr. William Shaw and his team worked to save Mrs. Gerney's crushed legs, surgeons were operating in an adjacent room to reattach the nearly severed foot of one man and the severed hands of another.

Trauma patients may need the help of many surgical specialists: neurosurgeons, orthopedic surgeons, vascular (blood vessels) surgeons, plastic surgeons, and microsurgeons.

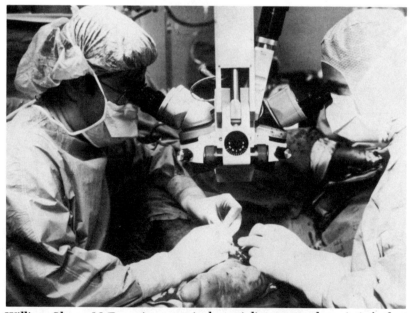

William Shaw, M.D., micro-surgical specialist re-attaches victim's foot and leg at Bellevue Hospital, New York City.

Even before Mrs. Gerney arrived at Bellevue, the team began preparing for her surgery. Work began just before 4:00 P.M. while police and paramedics continued to sustain her in the street. At about the same time, Dr. Shaw contacted the City Hospital Center at Elmhurst, Queens, where a man with a nearly severed foot was being treated. The man had been trapped under a trailer truck for two hours. When he arrived with his dangling foot at the Elmhurst hospital, the hospital followed the regulations, or protocols, that Dr. Shaw had circulated. (These clearly describe particular procedures.) The man arrived at Bellevue by helicopter at about 4:20 P.M., with his leg and damaged foot wrapped in plastic and surrounded by ice. He was taken to the eleventh floor for surgery.

Mrs. Gerney arrived at 6:05 P.M., after her epic six-hour ordeal. She suffered what Dr. Shaw describes as "bumper injuries." In trauma cases, the bone is sometimes broken, sometimes pulverized. Blood vessels and nerves are crushed, and muscles are severely damaged. Priorities must be decided immediately. Surgeons must decide who will work first and who will step aside. The team is choreographed perfectly, as surgeons move from one operating suite to the other as needed. The fifteen or more doctors work in the kind of harmony that comes only after long acquaintance. Dr. Shaw considers himself a catalyst rather than a captain of the team.

Bellevue's trauma team was formed ten years ago. Its goals remain the same. All the members work together on the same patient in nearly perfect coordination. They agree quickly about the most important problems and what should be done to treat them. The team performs hundreds of operations each year. Many patients arrive in medically outfitted helicopters. "Twenty years ago, damaged limbs were amputated because there was no hope of restoring function to the legs, arms, or hands. But over the past ten years, particularly in the last five, we have the concept that saving the function of a limb is just like saving a life," says Dr. Shaw.

The Bellevue operations on the three patients took nine hours altogether. Compare this with the reattachment of two severed limbs in a Boston hospital several years ago, which lasted thirty-six hours and made headlines.

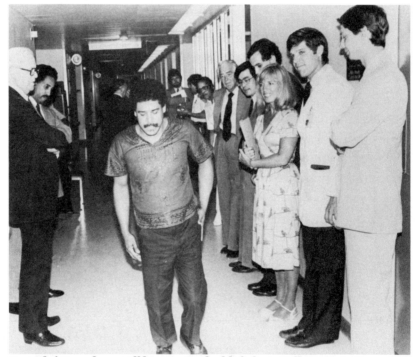

It works! Jose shows off his re-attached left foot. Bellevue's staff applauds.

EMERGENCY ROOM SERVICES

The emergency room at Bellevue resembles the one in the popular television series *St. Elsewhere* or any large municipal hospital. At almost any hour, EMS ambulance crews run in with stretchers or strapped-down agitated psychotics, stuporous alcoholics, violent teenagers, hemorrhaging gunshot or stab-wound victims, gasping asthmatics, moaning mothers in labor, and bruised and battered men and women. The EMS crews are often accompanied by police officers. Residents, nurses, and aides shout questions and answers across the static of the public address system, and hysterical relatives grieve in five different languages.

Oblivious to the apparent confusion and clamor, a young doctor quietly stands by a monitor reading an electrocardiogram (EKG). This tracing shows the heart action of a patient being transported to Bellevue by ambulance. This is the telemetry unit used by EMS to relay paramedical information from the street to the base hospital station. The EKG informs the doctor of the patient's current heart status. Paramedics can communicate by telephone, too, if the telemetry fails for any reason. All information is recorded for medical and legal purposes.

Walter Le Strange, Education Coordinator of the Emergency Care Institute, expands on this point: "Information is exchanged between the street or field and Bellevue. When the patient arrives, medical staff are ready to institute a treatment program; in part, based on medical data already received and recorded. Years ago, staff had to wait until the patient arrived and was examined and tests done before treatment could begin. Now treatment begins in the street and many more lives are saved." Dr. Lewis Goldfrank and Mr. Le Strange work with others directing and supervising the training of paramedics in a school located in the hospital.

Computers in the Emergency Room

As the director of one of the busiest emergency rooms in the country, Dr. Lewis Goldfrank foresees the computer making an even greater impact on health care as equipment is made smaller and more portable. If CAT scanners could be put into smaller devices, diagnoses could be made on the spot and the patient moved to the best hospital for that problem.

In New York City, hospital administrators know the location of heart, transplant, head trauma, and microsurgery centers. Transport to these centers is routine and an institutionalized procedure. When faced with more subtle problems, however, valuable time may be lost.

Dr. Goldfrank says that fifty years ago, when a doctor and a nurse responded to an ambulance request, they probably left the hospital and went out to render service. But they could render very little service or make few assessments because they were unable to take much equipment with them. Today, we have personnel with less training but who can use very capable technology. In the future, paraprofessionals or trained aids are likely to continue, but with improved capabilities made possible by computers and other technological devices.

Bed census is another area where the computer can be used. Procedure up to now has been to take the patient to the nearest hospital. Under this system, crowded emergency rooms and filled beds could cause a delay in assessment and treatment, which may endanger a patient's life. With the use of a computer, patients would be sent to the appropriate hospital. For example, a sick child may be sent to a hospital across town, although there is a hospital much nearer to the child's home. But EMS would know in advance that the more distant hospital had pediatric beds available. An abdominal gunshot wound would be treated similarly. In this case, the individual would need the services of an operating room, and the hospital would be alerted and prepared for the patient. Initial assessment would be done in the street and in the ambulance, thus saving precious moments in the treatment program.

Early diagnosis, which improves prehospital management, would also improve with greater use of computers. A paramedic treating a diabetic could, through blood and urine analyses, get a glucose, or sugar, level and begin insulin changes in the ambulance. Even serious illnesses such as cardiac arrests or severe heart attacks may be managed more effectively with the availability of blood test results at any early stage.

Dr. Goldfrank also predicts computer storage information on a national scale. "Everyone would be identified by name, birth date, and social security number. Previous hospitalizations, known illnesses, and allergy history would be entered too. So, if John Doe of San Diego collapses while visiting Philadelphia, the EMS picking him up would merely enter the identifying information and on relay learn that John Doe has a history of epilepsy and takes medication regularly. This information would permit medical personnel to respond immediately and rationally to the patient's symptoms. One could easily recognize the difference between a fainting spell, insulin shock, or hysteria."

Both professional and lay people have expressed concern regarding confidentiality. Some people are reluctant to use their social security numbers for identification in applying for loans, bank mortgages, or even insurance policies. There is fear that even the most private information may become available to almost anyone. However, in most cases, sophisticated and improved coding is being used that will lessen this possibility. Dr. Goldfrank says, "Doctors are concerned about civil rights and confidentiality too. We may have the problem of deciding upon privacy versus appropriate health care. But I would guess that much of what we do in the hospital now could be compressed into microchips so that we could do it in the field. So saving a life may take priority over confidentiality."

Is it possible that fifty years from now someone might have a CAT scan small enough to be carried around in a jacket pocket and operatable at most anywhere? "Oh yes," says Dr. Goldfrank. "But again, in another hundred years, doctors may return to making house calls since that little 'black bag' will contain everything. One must remember why people went to the hospital in the first place. It was for the technology!"

Research in Emergency Care

Because poison cases need emergency care, many specialists believe that more research in the field of toxicology will take place in the next ten years. Other research is concentrating on the study of chemical irritants, allergic reactions, and toxic fallout—all of which pollute the environment.

Most physicians who work in emergency care agree that what is done in the receiving hospital now will be processed in the future in a sophisticated outfitted van—an improvement on the highly publicized type currently used by the Boston Emergency Medical Center. This would eliminate the hours that people waste in emergency rooms. What is currently done in helicopter transport would be appropriate for ambulance services. In the former, all medical data are computerized and displayed on a screen. Here, the "big board," which is a large lighted screen, shows the patient's estimated time of arrival (ETA), name, address, age, sex, social security number, vital signs (including temperature, pulse rate, respiration, and blood pressure), all test results, medication prescribed, oxygen therapy, cardiac history, and possible bed location.

There is a new use of helicopters in Louisville, Kentucky— the Jewish Hospital's Skycare Service. This hospital has one of the country's largest cardiovascular programs, annually treating thousands of patients with cardiac diseases. It has established the first hospital-based helicopter ambulance service in Kentucky.

Cruising at 147 miles per hour and serving patients within a 150-nautical-mile radius of Louisville, Skycare covers the states of Illinois, Kentucky, Indiana, Ohio, Tennessee, and West Virginia. The helicopter is capable of landing in a seventy-five-foot-diameter area (one hundred feet at night) that is free from overhead wires and ground clutter. A nurse with critical-care and emergency department experience, a

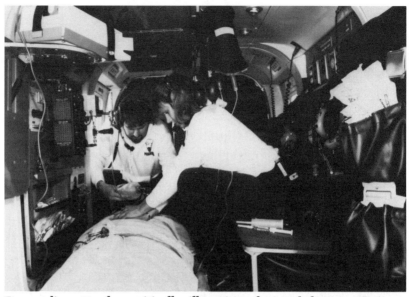

Paramedics attend a critically ill patient during helicopter flight to hospital.

paramedic who has completed Emergency Air Ambulance training, and a pilot make up the crew. Both medical personnel have completed training in advanced cardiac life support and advanced trauma life support measures.

Skycare is available twenty-four hours a day, seven days a week. A liftoff fee of $100 is charged, plus $4.50 for each nautical mile from the Jewish Hospital's seventh-floor heliport until return. Fees are billed to the patients and/or their insurance carriers.

In one eleven-month service period, the main categories of patients transported were cardiac (24 percent), multiple trauma (17.6 percent), hand and other trauma (15.6 percent), head and/or spinal cord injuries (11 percent), and neurological (10 percent). A recently published study in the *Journal of the American Medical Association* underscores the significant impact of helicopter ambulances. The research compared 140 patients transported to a trauma center by land ambulance with 150 carried to the same facility by helicopter. Fifty-two percent fewer patients died later in the group carried by the helicopter. Dr. David Holland, medical director of Skycare, adds, "Here the ultimate outcome of patients was positively affected in 43 percent of the cases. In 14 percent of the cases, the patient's condition actually improved during transport. Saving lives, alleviating pain and suffering, and improving patients' chances for recovery all tell the real Skycare story."

EMS systems and their physicians have played a dominant role in disaster planning and the evacuation and relocation of hospitalized patients, trauma resuscitation, rape, and child and spouse abuse. Much of this success was computer aided. The recent earthquakes in Mexico City illustrated how highly skilled technicians could use very sophisticated technology to locate hundreds of people successfully, some of whom had been buried for days. Problem solving is an essential ingredient of street medicine or the emergency medicine of the future. Computers are designed to solve problems. They provide a vast, detailed data bank from which to extract a solution to a problem.

Burn Centers

Another important part of emergency care is treatment for the burned patient. Immediate and life supporting care that restores lost body fluids and chemicals and prevents infection is essential. Around the country, burn centers have been established to provide the special care these patients need if they are to survive. An example is Jack Ryan, twenty-eight, who suffered second and third degree burns over half of his body when a boiler exploded in his apartment building. He was taken to New York Hospital Medical Center's Burn Center. Although it will be months before Jack recovers, he is well on the way to rehabilitation. He will need minimal skin grafts because he was given such excellent care before admission to the hospital.

Recently, Massachusetts General Hospital in Boston reported a medical marvel: the story of eight-year-old Glen Selby and his six-year-old brother, Jamie. They survived horrible burns over 97 percent of their bodies in a fire in their home in Casper, Wyoming. Burns as extensive as these are normally fatal, and death is slow and painful. Even more outstanding, Glen and Jamie's chances for normal lives are excellent, thanks to doctors at Massachusetts General. The doctors took what little healthy skin remained and used it to grow sheets of new skin in the laboratory for grafting over the burned areas.

Weather Emergencies

At times, it is the natural environment or even the weather that presents the challenge. Several years ago, the city of Miami, Florida, faced the challenge of providing emergency services to the thousands of citizens who live on houseboats, yachts, and fishing craft. The solution—which caught the attention of the worlds of rescue, firefighting, and boating— was an amphibious fire truck. The basis of this unit is an army light amphibious rescue craft combined with a super space-aged pump. On land, the truck does thirty miles an hour. On the water, it travels ten miles an hour and can deliver 3000 gallons of water.

The amphibious fire truck is manned by a special tactics team, consisting of EMTs who are trained to give emergency first-response treatment to boaters and any victims needing medical aid in areas where normal rescue paramedic response is not possible. The truck is also invaluable in rescuing citizens from low-lying areas around Miami after hurricanes or floods. It can respond to fire or medical emergencies that previously only helicopters could reach. However, because of their size, helicopters were of limited use for firefighting and rescue evacuation. The Light Amphibious Rescue Craft (LARK) is another advancement to upgrade the saving of lives through innovation brought on by challenge. Increased sophistication of equipment will continue to contribute to improved trauma and emergency care. High technology, including computers, is an ever-expanding tool of medicine.

CHAPTER 2

Scalpel! Clamp! Sponge!

This dramatic request is made often by doctors, both in movies and in real life, in thousands of operating rooms across the country. There is something mysterious and even scary about operating rooms. Standing above the completely covered patient, the blue-, yellow-, green-, or pink-garbed men and women speak softly as they quietly move about doing their special tasks. In intensive care suites, there is so much equipment attached to the patient that he or she is barely visible. But this equipment is saving lives.

Watching major surgery completed in less than thirty minutes on television only increases the image of spectacular magic. But what really happens in those brightly lit rooms has little to do with magic. Highly skilled, hard-working, dedicated medical professionals are using new tools and new procedures to help them do things that were thought impossible a few years ago. These new technological advances have created a need for special units in hospitals.

INTENSIVE CARE UNITS

In most large hospitals, there may be as many as six intensive care units. Some care for patients who are recovering from surgery and trauma. Others accept patients with heart problems or who are recovering from heart surgery, including heart transplants. Some are for patients with nerve damage or neurological conditions. And there are units for babies and small children. A visit to Lincoln Hospital, a large city institution in the Bronx, New York, shows how one of these new tools—the computer—helps the staff care for critically ill patients.

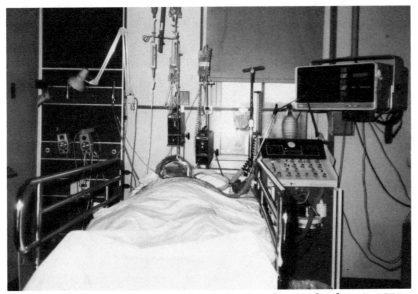

A critically ill patient receives the benefit of modern technology in ICU at Presbyterian Hospital, New York City.

Technology and the Critically Ill

Lincoln Hospital is a huge, red-brick complex. Part of the hospital was opened in 1976 and is therefore fairly new. Even so, its problems are old and familiar. This municipal hospital serves the poor, the illegal alien, the aged, and various ethnic groups of Central America—many of whom still live in burned-out, deserted shells of aging, city-owned buildings. *"Espanol es habla aqui"* appears beside every English sign. One can walk through the large complex for an hour without hearing English spoken once. Emergency rooms, clinic services, and admission offices are constantly busy and crowded. As a result, the surgical suites on two floors maintain a daily census of 130 patients of all ages. Eight operating rooms are busy around the clock.

In the Intensive Care Units (ICUs), tests performed on the patients appear on the small television-like screens next to their beds. These readings permit the staff to know the exact condition of the patients' systems at any given moment. Results of earlier completed tests are also stored in a bedside computer and can be recalled at any time. According to Dr. William Stahl, Chief of Surgery at Lincoln, the computer takes the data, puts them in practical language, and displays them. It says, "Here is your information. Now use it." Over a twenty-four-hour period, much information on a critically ill patient must be kept at hand. The computer makes this possible.

Lincoln, like Bellevue Hospital, is a trauma center. Many of the patients in the surgical suites are victims of fires,

Bruce Towe, Ph.D. with ICU monitor that he developed for Samaritan Health Service in Phoenix, Arizona.

building collapses, and automobile accidents. Others are there as a result of gun fights, holdups, and stabbings. They are brought to the hospital in ambulances equipped with the latest technology. When there is a major disaster, ambulances and helicopters take patients to several hospitals. This can create a problem in record-keeping. A computer could help physicians cope with this problem. The doctors would be able to tell how many seriously injured patients, in general, actually arrive at the city's sixteen certified trauma centers. A computerized trauma registry may be the answer.

Lynn P. Phillips, R.N., Coordinator of Trauma and Emergency Service at Ohio Valley Medical Center in Wheeling, West Virginia, developed such a registry. To simplify data collection, she uses the hospital-based computer. Nurses in a special unit are asked to follow trauma cases and to put together the necessary information. After their discharge, patients' records are sent to the trauma nurse coordinator to be included in the Trauma Registry. This registry can be kept for years and provides immediate data without relying on medical records—each of which has to be read individually. Reading records is time-consuming, and time is money.

Plans are being made to include a medical data base to store additional information and to eliminate the need for paper records. The system will be useful for administrators needing future data to study and will provide statistics for regional EMSs.

At Parkland Memorial Hospital in Dallas, Texas, their ultra-modern ICU consists of cubicles—each with four to six beds, fanned out in a semicircle in front of the nurses' station. Each bed is screened off by fiber glass ceiling-to-floor sliding doors. Although the patient is visible at all times, there is a sense of privacy. More importantly, the danger of crossinfection between patients is lessened. Hanging above each bed is a small computer screen. Patients have colored discs attached to their bodies, which constantly measure their vital signs, including blood pressure, heart rate, respiration, and temperature. These discs have sensors that convert forms of energy such as heat, light, and pressure into electrical impulses. These impulses are then transmitted to a computer, which then analyzes all the information for easy reading on

A mini lab in a Surgical Cardiac Intensive Care Unit permits staff to make frequent and instant tests for blood gases of their patients.

the screens above the patients' beds. Blood loss and urine output can be measured, too. The computer also uses a data storage system that can give not only the activity of a patient's heart on a minute-to-minute basis but can retrieve heart rate readings from a previous day. In this way, comparisons can be made. If an irregularity occurs, or if a disc or lead attached to the patient falls off or becomes loose, the computer flashes an alert immediately with a ringing alarm.

Monitoring Heart Action

Some hospitals, such as Columbia Presbyterian Hospital in New York, have intensive care units for patients who have heart problems and for those who have had heart surgery, including heart transplants. The electrocardiogram (EKG) plays an important part in the care and treatment of a person with heart problems. This machine gives a graphic reading of the beats and rhythm of the heart. This test is an important part of an adult's physical examination, especially if he or she is older than thirty-five. Sometimes a patient may need a series of readings of the heartbeat. By monitoring a patient for a full twenty-four-hour period, doctors can detect possible serious conditions such as heart block. Heart block occurs when the heart fails to conduct impulses normally to its chambers, and it can lead to a rapid heartbeat or heart attack. EKG testing only records twelve to fifteen seconds of heart activity, but the computer can analyze a patient's tapes over a full day and then tabulate the frequency of each heartbeat

Nurses and doctors observe patients in Cardiac ICU at Presbyterian Hospital, New York City.

type. Dr. Coromilas, staff doctor at the hospital, points out that certain things may happen only once in a twenty-four-hour period, which a routine EKG test could miss. The computer can classify each electrical signal of the heart as well as the time it occurred, its shape, area, and height.

Another type of heart-watching is done by telemetry. This technique is used to observe heart action from a distance. It was mentioned in the first chapter as a means of informing emergency room doctors of the condition of a patient's heart while he or she is still in transit to the hospital. Telemetry is also used after patients leave the Cardiac Intensive Care Unit (CICU) to continue their recuperation in general care units elsewhere in the hospital. They are kept in touch with the

Parkland Memorial Hospital, Dallas, Texas Telemetry Station showing individual tracings (four) and all four on one monitor screen.

CICU staff through this type of monitoring. The patient carries a small monitor in an over-the-shoulder-type case, much like a camera. The wireless unit picks up the electrical signals of the heartbeat and relays their wave length and patterns to the desktop computer in the Telemetry Center. The television-like screens there and on the patients' floors display the recording. If there is an irregularity, it is immediately obvious. Frequently, a lead can be dislodged while a patient is active, such as while shaving, eating, changing position, or performing self-care. The screen at the nurses' station displays the irregularity and an alarm sounds. The Telemetry Center telephones the nurse regarding the irregularity, because they see it, too. The lead can be replaced by the floor nurse immediately and the recording continues.

Respirators Help Patients Breathe

A computerized respirator that collects and stores data is often used for treating seriously ill trauma patients in intensive care units. Often, injuries received in a car collision, a multiple car crash, an explosion, or an event such as the crane that fell on Mrs. Gerney result in chest and spinal damage associated with difficulty in breathing. Respirators are used to ease this situation. Air may be forced through a tube in the patient's nose or through a tracheotomy, which is a surgical opening in the throat. A controlled stream of air passes through to the patient's lungs by way of the respirator. The respirator's computer supervises the breathing in response to the particular needs of the patient. It records changes in

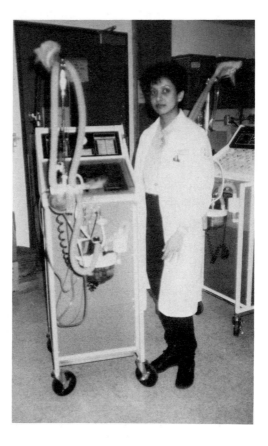

Paduma is a R.R.T. (Registered Respiratory Therapist). This is the computerized respirator used in the Surgical Cardiac Intensive Care Unit (SCICU) at Presbyterian Hospital.

airway pressure, and unusually high or low readings trip an alarm.

As the patient's condition improves, he or she is weaned away from dependence on the respirator. Automatically, the air supply is reduced to encourage the patient's lungs to expand and contract normally. As the computer senses the patient's growing strength, it provides increasingly less artificial help until the patient is able to breathe unaided.

Patient Education and Intensive Care Units

Historically, the intensive care unit was not believed to be the best environment for patient education and discharge planning. These activities were usually done later, after the patient was transferred from the unit to a general medical or surgical area of the hospital. This situation has changed drastically under new federal regulations that limit a patient's stay in the hospital. Hospitalization until recovery is out. Discharge prior to full recuperation is in.

Patients over the age of sixty-five have been most adversely affected by the new system. They use hospitals at 3.5 times the rate of those under the age of sixty-five. Although this group represents only 11 percent of the population, they account for 29 percent of personal health care expenditure.

Critical-care nurses are now responsible for an increasing number of patients who are acutely ill, older, and hospitalized for a shorter time. For many patients, critical care may be the only hospital area they encounter and the only setting where discharge preparation of any kind is available to them. Critical-care nurses will need a knowledge of geriatric nursing and will have to prepare elderly patients for self-care at home and how to use community resources effectively. Technology, which shortened hospitalization, will follow these patients home. Computerized pacemakers, telemetry, automatic feeding and infusion systems, portable respirators, and self-testing of blood and urine along with self-administered blood pressure taking will be used in the home care trend.

Caring for Cancer Patients

Memorial Sloan-Kettering Hospital, a nationally known New York hospital, provides for the care and treatment of patients with a variety of cancers. A critical-care specialist at this hospital, Dr. Graziano C. Carlon, says: "The basic function of the [computer] is to do repetitive work that is routine and monotonous. The computer can schedule orders, check them for accuracy, alert the physician to incompatibilities and contradictions, automatically set time intervals, and remind nurses to give patients their medications." If a nurse goes off duty and forgets to administer a medication or sign an order, the computer will not forget, and the medication will be given by another nurse.

Dr. Carlon reminds us that the computer should serve the user. "The computer does not interfere with the doctor–patient relationship. It supports what doctors or nurses do."

Dr. Carlon also believes that another important function of the computer is to help make future plans for the use of the unit based on collected data. He is faced with this dilemma: "How do we provide the best care and provide it in an efficient manner?" His research hopes to find ways to do this. It is the beginning of a long-range project that promises to identify procedures, time, and effort used for procedures and collect relevant medical care information. Dr. Carlon feels the investigation may answer two important ethical questions. "We must learn more about assignment of patients to these units. And, more importantly, we must distinguish between which is worthwhile: 'prolongation of life' or 'delay of death' in this extremely costly service." The computer will

29

also assist in making the most productive allocation of personnel within the intensive care unit.

Critically Ill Babies and Children

What is happening today in pediatrics intensive care units
is really miraculous. Ten years ago doctors did not believe
that young children could be helped with the respirators and
special techniques that are used for adults. Dr. Florence
Nolan is director of the new Pediatric Intensive Care Unit at
New York Hospital, which opened in 1984. It is the most
modern of its kind in the United States. Bed capacity is
twelve, with eight beds set aside for extremely ill children.
When the unit joins EMS, trauma patients will be transferred
here as well.

In this unit, new equipment is everywhere. All around are
state-of-the-art monitors with computers. The monitors "talk
to each other." Dr. Nolan explains: "If a patient in bed four is
being cared for by a nurse and something happens to a
patient in a totally different room, the monitor beside the
patient to whom the nurse is giving care will start alarming. A
readout on the screen will show the pressure, EKG irregular-
ities, or whatever is causing the alarming condition in that
other room. If nobody has recognized the situation or if no
one is at that child's bedside, this nurse can respond or alert
someone else to the trouble."

Dr. Nolan tells about other exciting plans for the new unit.
Staff will be able to develop a cardio-pulmonary profile,
which shows heart and lung pictures, to show moment-to-

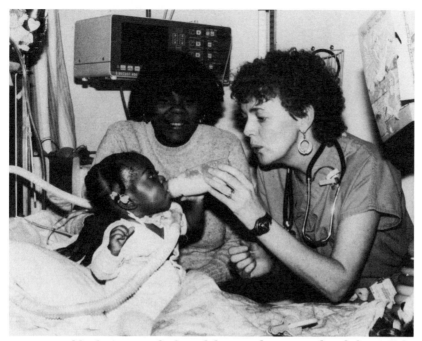

One-year-old Shavonne Clark and her mother get a hand from Judy Douglas, R.N. in Pediatric Surgery at Presbyterian Hospital.

moment changes in data of children in shock, postoperative children, or children in coma. These changes would be in the children's circulation systems, respiratory systems, and cardiac output.

The new monitors not only measure vital signs but up to or as many as four to five pressures on each child. This may sound excessive, but some children not only need regular blood pressure monitoring, but readings of the pressure in their veins and the arteries in the brain, and even their windpipes, to help them recover from their acute illnesses.

There are a few bed stations that have even greater monitoring capabilities. One is the isolation room, which was designed for the greatest amount of monitoring capabilities. An AIDS victim could be cared for in there, if necessary.

What about the people who work with critically ill infants and children? What are they like? Dr. Nolan talks about the physicians first. "I've been here seven years and am board certified in pediatrics and cardiology." Her training as both a pediatrician and a heart specialist provides her with the background to take care of the very sick children, as well as the specific ability to deal with heart surgery, heart functional problems, and the invasive techniques that a doctor learns as a cardiologist. Placing catheters and other monitoring lines in patients' bodies for the purpose of stabilizing them is one example of the expertise a cardiologist needs. Dr. Nolan's associate is a pediatrician and a specialist in intensive care for children.

Formal teaching conferences for residents are held twice a week. Postgraduate level staff, including senior residents in pediatrics, are on the unit at all times. Four serve during the day and two serve at night on a rotating basis, so someone who is familiar with the cases is on all the time. This is important to parents, who are allowed to visit their children at almost any hour.

The nursing staff—special, dedicated men and women with more than five years' service—promote positive family communication. Parents feel reassured by the care given their children by the nurses.

What makes 1986 different from 1975? Dr. Nolan responds. "The major difference in care for children as opposed

Jug Kyog Kwon, 5, and Suk Jo Mok, 4, from South Korea traveled halfway around the world to have heart surgery at Bellevue Hospital in New York City. Never expecting to live another year, they now look forward to normal lives as the result of corrective surgery. (New York Daily News)

to ten years ago is that one can take care of them. A doctor doesn't have to stand by helplessly using traditional treatment and second-guessing in terms of lung, heart, and kidney function. One can actually measure all of these special characteristics the same way as in adult patients."

There are exciting days ahead for the unit. A pediatrician who is also an anesthesiologist is to join the unit. So, eventually, the unit will have three specialists—a cardiologist, an intensivist, and an anesthesiologist—all of whom are trained in pediatrics. Dr. Nolan stops to look around the large, well-lit, attractively decorated unit with its shiny new equipment,

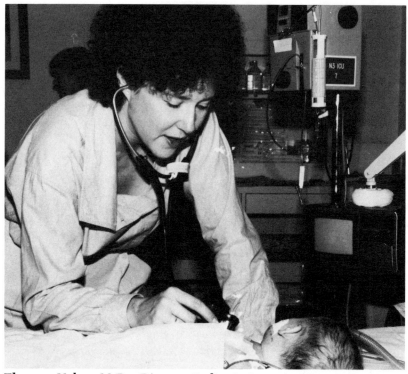

Florence Nolan, M.D., Director Pediatric Intensive Care Unit at New York Hospital Medical Center, New York caring for one of the critically ill infants in the new unit.

able staff, children, and parents. "Although I do not like to rely on technology alone, it has been a helpful tool. I think the major difference in our ICU is having experienced physicians guiding the care of these children. They know what complications can occur, how to stop them, and how to use the technology for the children's benefit. The machines are nice, but if you don't know how to use them they're of no help to you," concludes Dr. Nolan.

Staff and Patients Cope with Stress

Many nurses feel that operating-room and critical-care staff are subjected to stress and pressure situations that do not exist in most other patient-care areas in the hospital. Nurses' knowledge and assessment skills, technical expertise, problem-solving and decision-making skills are in constant use. The computer has relieved them of some of the personal pressures and anxieties leading to the often heard complaint of burnout.

Ms. Rowena Woodley, R.N., Nursing Care Clinician, supervises the Surgical Cardiac Intensive Care Unit at Columbia Presbyterian Hospital. She depends upon computers. "In my area, computers simplify the paper work and give nurses more time to interact with patients. The nurses can do bedside nursing, which is their real mission. It's a timesaver and permits the nurse to eliminate routine, mechanical procedures and concentrate more on patients' needs."

Despite these efforts, many patients do feel stressful in the unit. "When I was admitted to the intensive care unit, I was too sick to notice anything. But as I began to recover, many things bothered me," a former patient reveals. Her story is repeated by many other patients. The noise level, at times, can be quite high. There are staff conversations, equipment being moved, patients being transferred in and out of the unit, distressed patients, and telephones ringing. Patients complain also about the lack of privacy and the ceiling lights, which are always burning brightly. Often they are disturbed by what they imagine is happening to other patients in the unit and the sobbing of grieving relatives. Because of the need to respond rapidly to all situations, patients may be excluded from decision-making and the care being rendered. The unknown and unfamiliar are always frightening. With increases in staff and staff training in interpersonal relations, it is to be hoped that patients' complaints will be less as stressful situations are eradicated.

ANESTHESIOLOGY AND COMPUTERS

In recent years, some operating rooms have been experimenting with a system designed to assist the anesthetist with record-keeping. During surgery, this specialist keeps a detailed written account of his or her activities and of the patient's condition. As the practice of anesthesia has become more complex, so has the task of record-keeping. This accounting is probably the most comprehensive document in the patient's chart. Complete, accurate, legible, and up-to-the-minute recording is vital. Yet the task of data entry is greatest during the period when the anesthetist is too busy to be involved with the record.

Computers can help automate the anesthesia record. There are some difficulties, however, such as limited methods for entering drug injections or blood transfusions. Dr. Andrew J. Sarnat, Clinical Professor of Anesthesiology at the University of California in San Diego, and his staff have developed an experimental system of data entry based on computerized speech recognition (CSR). This new technology uses a computer that "understands" words spoken into a microphone. Dr. Sarnat's experimental system is called Entry to the Anesthesia Record by Speech (EARS). The program works in the following way. "It is an isolated-word, speaker-dependent system which uses a predefined vocabulary of three hundred and fifty words." Each word must first be pronounced by the anesthetist to train the computer to the sounds of a particular voice. After that, data are entered by spoken words separated by brief pauses and organized into brief sentences. Completed sentences are then read back to the anesthetist by a speech synthesizer to check voice recognition. Some flexibility is built in, so that frequently used phrases can be used on cue. An example of such a phrase is "Breathing nitrous oxide three liters per minute."

Dr. Sarnat warns us that the accuracy of EARS has not been measured, but its performance in the operating room seems acceptable. Future plans are to incorporate a new CSR for better recognition accuracy. But EARS holds promise for the future.

Victor Zue, assistant professor of electrical engineering and computer science at Massachusetts Institute of Technology (MIT), believes the real solution to Dr. Sarnat's problem is somewhere in the next century. "Remaining problems are being approached one or two dimensions at a time. MIT is working toward a system that would not understand continuous speech but could identify 10,000 or 20,000 words spoken by different speakers. Another system would understand continuous speech from different speakers but would have a limited vocabulary such as a few digits perhaps."

The ultimate goal might be a computer that people talk to

as they would talk to another person, or a computer that would automatically take dictation. Both still seem very far off.

LASERS SHORTEN HOSPITALIZATION

Lasers, the ultimate beam, are on the cutting edge of the technologies. They are changing medicine and are making same-day surgery faster, safer, and more comfortable for patients. Lasers have come a long way from their science fiction roots in *The War of the Worlds,* in which H. G. Wells frightened his readers with his description of the laserlike heat rays used by Martian invaders.

Lasers have a specific wavelength and an intense and precisely focused beam. This pinpoint light can cut through skin without harming it. Lasers seal blood vessels as they cut, thereby allowing very little blood loss. The high temperature of the laser sterilizes the site of the operation, reducing possible infection. Lasers are also good in places that are hard to reach such as the inside of the nose, ears, and genitals.

For these and other reasons, lasers have made "walk-away" same-day surgery a reality. In 1981, fewer than 10 percent of operations in the United States were performed on an outpatient basis. In 1986, about 30 percent of all surgical procedures are done this way, and by 1990, this could easily rise to 40 percent. Climbing hospital costs, the desire for patients to take an active role in their own care, and advances in anesthesia and endoscopy have all stimulated the demand for this type of service. Endoscopy is the inspection of body organs or cavities using a tubelike instrument with a light that has the ability to probe into the inner recesses of the colon and remove polyps without major surgery. President Reagan had this type of surgery.

Operations done in this way—cataract removal, hernia repair, bone and joint surgery, biopsies, female sterilization, and tonsillectomy—are saving time and money for thousands of people. These day-hospital centers are particularly suited for the young and the elderly. For young children, outpatient surgery lessens the trauma of separation from parents. The elderly often fear hospitals and think of hospitalization as a one-way trip. Attractive to people who are generally healthy, the centers will continue to draw increasing numbers of patients.

CHAPTER 3

New Hope for
New Lives

The year 1986 brought continuing increases in the use of computers as an important arm of medical practice. One major example of how computers work with new techniques is found in the care of newborn infants, especially in the support of high-risk premature babies and other sick young children.

INFANT TRANSPORT

The intermittent shrillness of the siren cuts sharply through the cold air, and one's attention is drawn toward the sleek, yellow-and-white ambulance snaking its way through cars, trucks, and buses on a busy, narrow downtown street in New York City. Printed on the sides of the ambulance are the words INFANT TRANSPORT.

Inside, a nurse practitioner and supervisor of the service attends to a tiny infant. About two hours earlier, the little girl was born in her mother's Wall Street law office, two months premature. She is being transported from downtown Beekman Hospital to St. Vincent's Hospital, where she will get the special care needed to sustain her life. Because her tiny lungs are not fully matured, she was placed on a respirator at Beekman Hospital. The nurse monitors the flow of oxygen in a steady stream to the baby's lungs, which helps her to breathe. The baby lies in a heated incubator that provides a warm environment and maintains her body heat. This is normal practice. Equipment on the transport includes cardio-respiratory (heart and breathing) monitors; a suction machine to clear mucus from infants' mouths and throats; small I.V. pumps for administering intravenous fluids; a complete emergency kit; and extensive resuscitation equipment.

Later in her office at Bellevue Hospital, Nurse Barbara Greitzer talks about the service: "The service has been around for many years, but the new technology has made tremendous changes in the way we move babies and the type of babies able to be moved. Other changes include the care that it is now possible to offer babies during the trip. At times, the trip can last more than an hour. That is a significant amount of time for a tiny, sick baby."

If the baby develops a problem in transit, the nurse or technician can radio the center for help. So far, the staff have not had such an emergency. Although the city is large, most babies are transported to hospitals within the borough in which they live. This makes visiting by parents easier and more frequent. The average trip from hospital to hospital is completed within thirty minutes. Even so, the transport is equipped to maintain an infant indefinitely in case traffic is snarled.

Although infant survival rate is excellent, Dr. Yucel Atakent, Assistant Medical Director of Infant Transport Service, continues to seek ways to improve it. "We recently analyzed our data on infants who had been transported by our service during the years 1977 and 1981. These infants weighed less than 1000 grams, or 2.2 pounds. They were transported from general hospitals to tertiary units or medical centers like Bellevue Hospital. The data are useful in studying the subtle effects and possible clues to stabilization, and this certainly will affect survival rates." Computers are used for data collection and analyses at the center.

Of the 1000 babies transported each year, 10 percent are below 1000 grams in weight. The transport serves fifty-two hospitals in the five boroughs of New York City and transports about 10 percent of all live births in the city.

A potential use of computers is in the actual transport. Dr. Atakent cites this possibility: "Suppose a nurse is sent out to pick up an infant and discovers that the baby has heart problems? The nurse may need to relay the data to us for diagnosis and treatment. Telemetry would be very useful in this case. The practice could correct possible errors that can occur through verbal communication made when using the radio, too."

SAVING THE TINY ONES

Doctors and nurses are beginning to enjoy the new and enlarged neonatology unit on the eighth floor of Bellevue Hospital. Dr. Michael Graff, assistant professor in Pediatrics at New York University Medical Center, is in charge of the nursery.

Bellevue's newborn unit receives 250 to 300 admissions each year. The majority of babies taken care of in the unit are premature. Although Bellevue Hospital has a premature rate of 9 to 10 percent of all live births, this is not significantly different from other institutions across the country. However, Bellevue does serve a high-risk group; many of the women who deliver there have received little prenatal care, and some are only teenagers when they deliver. Both the lack of prenatal care and the incidence of teenage pregnancy are factors that increase the likelihood of delivering prematurely or having a complicated pregnancy.

Dr. Graff says, "Technological advancements are perhaps the most important factor in our ability to preserve the lives of the smallest and sickest babies. Ten years ago, saving a baby who weighed less than 1000 grams was considered impossible, while today we consider this routine. Today, our ability to save infants weighing as little as 600 grams bears a direct relationship to changes in technology."

There is a five-bed intensive care unit here. Modern equipment and more space are improving care of these infants. With the completion of the Neonatal Intensive Care

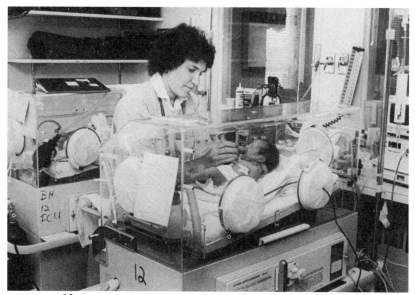

Janet Stickle, R.N., prepares an infant to leave his isolette in the Neonatal Intensive Care Unit for the first time since his birth.

Unit, (NICU) the census has increased to twenty. Eventually, the unit will be able to accommodate twenty-five babies with anticipated additions to the nursing staff. "Right now, the limit of our abilities to save babies appears to be those who weigh between 450 to 500 grams, which is about 25 to 26 weeks gestation, or development. To save a baby of less than this amount of development would require a new breakthrough in technology."

"Every year, there are advancements in technology which provide hope for people stricken with terminal illnesses. One widely publicized case was an infant whom we watched grow for twelve years." Dr. Graff is speaking of David, the Bubble Boy: "When he was born, there was no hope that he could survive in our environment. David was born without anti-bodies and was not able to develop these vital substances, so he was immune deficient. Human beings have antibodies within their bodies which provide protection and resistance to disease. Treatment with red bone marrow is now helping children with this problem. Red bone marrow found in the bones of the head, vertebrae, ribs, femur, and other bones is important in the formation of white blood cells, the most active of infection fighters. David lived long enough to receive a then new and experimental treatment several years ago of bone marrow. Unfortunately, he died later because of a virus infection. But this doesn't mean that the next person with this disorder might not survive."

David, a bright, cheerful boy spent all but the last fifteen days of his twelve years in a sterile plastic bubble. Except for a brief excursion into the outside world in a "spacesuit" made for him by the Johnson Space Center in 1978, he never left either of the increasingly larger and more complicated bubbles that were his world—whether in the hospital or at home. Now children like David are treated while still infants or quite young, possibly using knowledge gained from David's case.

In Plymouth, Massachusetts, a boy was given bone marrow transplants shortly after birth. At five months, he was able to leave his isolation condition and go home to almost sterile conditions. Since it takes time to develop antibodies, the youngster's home was made as sterile as possible. The germs that normally are found in our homes and the outside world—to which most people are immune—could possibly have been overwhelming to the child's body.

At fifteen months, he ate his first banana. Fruit had previously been eliminated from his diet because of the danger of bacteria. Eating a banana was a sort of milestone.

New technology is helping to reduce the percentage of small babies who have lifelong handicaps, such as learning disabilities. Today, if a baby is larger than two pounds at birth, that baby has a very good chance of being normal. More than 90 percent of babies weighing more than this weight are normal when seen in follow-up examination. Prematurity itself does not result in a larger number of handicapped children. If 250 premature babies a year survive, only five to ten will have any handicap, according to Dr. Graff. The rest will be physically and mentally normal. Triplets were born at Bellevue in 1984. The smallest weighed less than two pounds and the largest 2.5 pounds. All three were seen recently in the follow-up clinic and are doing well.

Dr. Graff is completing research in bilirubin, which is an orange-colored or yellowish pigment in bile. It is carried to the liver by the blood. When bilirubin reaches a certain level in the infant's bloodstream, it can lead to brain damage. Many babies are born with a yellow tinge in their skin, because of a natural rise in bilirubin. Phototherapy or exposure to sunlight or artificial light is used to overcome this condition. Dr. Graff is trying to measure the amount of light each baby receives and make the dose more uniform. "Since we don't know how much light the babies are receiving when they are under phototherapy, this research will provide an additional tool for both the physician and the nurse caring for the infant. When the level of bilirubin appears to be rising, we place the babies under fluorescent light bulbs, which are

Premature infant receives phototherapy treatment.

predominantly blue in color. If the rise continues, we perform an exchange transfusion in which blood is withdrawn from the baby and replaced by a transfusion."

At Babies Hospital on the upper west side of Manhattan, Dr. John M. Driscoll, Jr., Director of the NICU, talks about the effect of technology on low birth-weight infants. "Technology, certainly in the form of monitoring, has contributed in a very important way to the care of the very low birth-weight infant. We can monitor vital signs constantly and get quality or first rate, accurate tracings. That sort of monitoring allows us to make additional observations along with the critical, clinical input of the nursing staff." Because multiple births commonly deliver prematurely, and Babies Hospital is

Nurse Levin observes patient monitor at her desk in the labor and delivery suite at Presbyterian Hospital, New York.

a large premature center, there is a high incidence of multiple birth among the admissions.

At Babies Hospital, premature babies weighing 1.5 pounds or less are automatically transferred to the NICU after they are stabilized and show normal vital signs in the Transitional Care Nursery. "It's an ideal arrangement. The sooner we can give these very sick babies the special care that they need, the better," says Jane McConcille, a former associate director of Maternal and Child Nursing. "Years ago, the premature nursery was the quietest place in the hospital, because there was so little we could do for these babies. Now, it's one of the busiest, because of the technology and skill we use to care for them." Multiple births of triplets, and even quadruplets in 1983, are not unusual in this hospital. In 1971, the Kienast quintuplets were born here.

Dr. Driscoll is joined in his concern for premature babies by his wife, Dr. Yvonne Driscoll, who is also a pediatrician. On another floor of the hospital, she and her staff are working on an important follow-up study. They are observing high-risk infants over a six-year period. These are infants who weighed 1.5 pounds or less at birth. They are looking for any neurological handicap and abnormal patterns of general development in these premature children. Data are collected, evaluated, and stored in the computer. Some networking is done with other programs studying premature children around the country and in Canada.

The Driscolls, parents of six children, find great satisfaction in saving and caring for these tiny, frail infants.

NEW HEART AND LUNG SUPPORT

Immediately after birth, the new infant takes control of his or her own breathing. The child's skin might be bluish in color. To save the baby from respiratory failure, the most common cause of death in newborns, the doctors now have an ally. Doctors at Babies Hospital now use a procedure that directly adds oxygen and removes carbon dioxide from the blood of a child for up to fourteen days. This therapy is called Extra Corporeal Membrane Oxygenation (ECMO) which means, literally, outside of the body oxygenated membranes.

The important part of the machine is the oxygenating device, which looks like a roll of paper towels made of very thin silicone rubber sheets. As blood passes over two silicone sheets that have oxygen flowing between them, it picks up oxygen and gives off carbon dioxide. ECMO gives the baby's

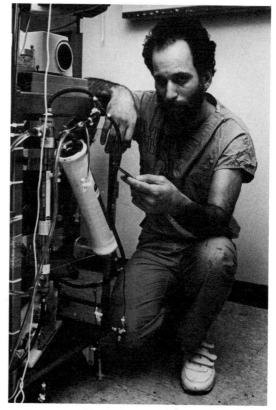

Dr. Charles Stolar with ECMO at Presbyterian Hospital, N.Y.—the machine that gives babies' hearts and lungs a chance to rest by adding oxygen and removing carbon dioxide directly from the blood.

lungs a chance to rest and heal, and also helps to minimize the amount of damage to the baby's delicate lungs caused by high oxygen concentrations and respirator pressures that are ordinarily used to help these infants breathe. Doctors use the therapy on premature infants and those who have a variety of breathing problems. These babies have conditions that cause pulmonary blood pressure to increase to dangerously high levels.

The change in the baby's condition is dramatic and quick. As the infant's condition improves, doctors wean the baby from the machine. The infant's natural ability to maintain an adequate level of oxygen in the blood gradually increases while on the machine, and the amount of freshly oxygenated blood from the bypass machine is reduced as the baby's lungs take over.

Babies Hospital is the only hospital in the New York, New Jersey, and Connecticut area that offers ECMO therapy and is a major referral center for newborns in the Northeast United States.

TECHNOLOGY AND MODERNIZATION

In other parts of the country, health professionals are joining technology with modernization. "No more babies born in elevators," says Dr. Reuben Adams, Chief of Obstetrics at Baylor University Medical School in Dallas, Texas. The new Obstetrical Unit, Labor and Delivery Suites, and Nursery are within one hundred yards of busy Gaston Avenue traffic. Each labor room has fetal monitoring facilities and a comfortable chair for the father-to-be. Near these rooms are the birthing and delivery suites. Here everything has been done to ensure operating-room sterility, yet the atmosphere is like home. A new mother cradling her ten-minute-old baby joins her family in a room very much like one in her own home. The bed is wooden, the linens colorful, and carpeting decorative. A few steps away is the nursery where newborns are carefully examined by doctors and nurses. When the babies are declared stabilized, they are transferred to the main nursery or NICU on another floor.

OUTPATIENT CARE

A recent project in New York City demonstrates how computers are helping to monitor and evaluate the pediatric care given to children at two municipal hospital clinics. This project has proved to be so successful that it is being extended to other hospitals. A computer issues printouts of clinic patients and the physicians who treated them. Staff can now identify who should have been hospitalized and who was not, and who was admitted unnecessarily.

The program, which only applies to outpatient pediatric care, was initially established at Kings County Hospital Center in Brooklyn in 1980 and at Metropolitan Hospital two years later, with the help of the Fund for City of New York, which is a private foundation. The cost has been less than a million dollars. It will be extended to three other municipal institutions. Under the program, uniform diagnoses and treatment procedures have been created for 85 percent of pediatric illnesses that are usually treated in a doctor's office or a hospital clinic—everything from a common cold to more serious life-threatening disorders. If a physician does not follow the mandated diagnosis and treatment procedures, the omission is recorded by the computer and the physician is compelled to defend the reasons for those actions to the medical supervisors. "In a way," Dr. Richard K. Stone, chief of Pediatrics at Metropolitan Medical Center says, "we are looking over doctors' shoulders with the help of a computer printout now."

A major result, hospital officials say, is the assurance that a patient will receive the same medical care from a young intern as he or she would from a more experienced attending physician. Continuity of excellent care assures a speedy recovery and a healthy child.

The program, called the *Computer-Assisted Pediatrics Protocol System,* has reduced the use of unnecessary drugs and diagnostic tests and encouraged the use of more appropriate treatment. For example, Dr. V. Rajagopal, Director of Outpatient Pediatrics at Kings County Hospital in Brooklyn, New York, says the computer-based monitoring system resulted in a sharp drop in the needless use of antibiotics in the treatment of simple respiratory illnesses. The level dropped from 28.2 percent in 1982 to 2.2 percent in 1983.

The new regulations establish step-by-step guidelines for the diagnosis and treatment of common childhood illnesses such as ear infection, pneumonia, asthma, fever, and seizures. Instead of using old hospital charts, a physician enters the case history and care plan with each step of a particular regulation on a code sheet that is fed into a central computer. The computer then generates regular reports detailing how physicians performed in relation to the stated guidelines.

SUDDEN INFANT DEATH

When an infant is born, doctors look for any signs that might point to a disease that might develop in the child. In most cases, the infant is fine. Occasionally, there is an indication of a problem, and then the infant is assessed through special tests, such as an electrocardiogram or an X-ray. In Sudden Infant Death Syndrome (SIDS), there is no way of telling that a newborn is at risk; the baby just dies.

SIDS, one of the leading killers of infants in the United States, claims nearly 10,000 lives a year. The only certainty about SIDS is that it most commonly strikes its tiny victims between two and four months of age.

"We don't know what leads to their deaths, so it's hard to design a test or a monitor to alert the parents before the infant dies," says Dr. Gabriel G. Haddad, a pediatrician at Babies Hospital. "These deaths are unexpected. When the baby is examined, the pediatrician finds nothing that would alert him or her to any abnormalities," he adds. "But that doesn't mean there's nothing wrong generically with these infants. It could be related to how the heart functions or how the brain interacts with the lungs or to the way the body uses energy at a time of stress."

Every time SIDS claims another infant's life, the parent's report is similar. The baby had just been fed and put to sleep. When the mother returned a half hour later to check on the baby, she found the infant blue, cold, and lifeless.

Marvin and Bianca Bakalar lost their first child to SIDS in 1981. He died two days before he would have turned two months old. Apparently in good health, Sebastian had seen the pediatrician the day before. "We felt helpless when our son died, especially because we didn't know why he died." At first, the Bakalars were afraid to build a family. But they now have two children. Their infant daughter, Chloe, is shown in the picture wearing her monitor.

Monitors are sometimes used on babies who might be at

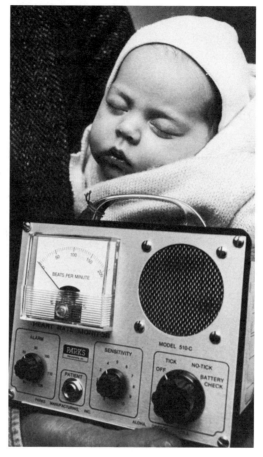

Sudden Infant Death (SID) baby wears monitor which alerts parents to changes in breathing.

risk for SIDS. Leads, similar to those used for heart tracing in electrocardiograms, are placed on the child's body. If the baby's respiration slows, becomes irregular, or even stops, the monitor sends out an alarm. Parents with high-risk babies—that is, in a family where SIDS has already occurred—are taught how to observe and record respirations, so many babies only need to wear the monitor at night when parents are asleep. Mr. Bakalar confirms this. "We keep a constant eye on Chloe. We check her chest and heartbeat all the time and only use the monitor at night."

There are no definite answers as to why these babies die. Yet, medical researchers are working on new studies and are accumulating a substantial amount of knowledge using new technology. Recently, over 250 scientists, physicians, and other health professionals from around the world participated in the first international research conference on SIDS held since 1974. The conference was convened because of the many new and exciting research leads that have emerged in recent years. The enthusiasm generated by the conference led to the creation of the National Center for the Prevention of Sudden Infant Death. Its purpose is to plan and support research.

Sudden Infant Death Syndrome remains our nation's leading killer of infants beyond two weeks of life. It leaves in its wake a confused trail of fear, guilt, and bewilderment. Today, however, there is hope. The day when SIDS can be prevented and its causes understood may be getting closer.

CHAPTER 4

The Greatest Gift of All

Every parent prays for a healthy baby. The first thing a happy mother does is to count the fingers and toes, in a quick examination of her new baby. Sometimes though there is a defect that the mother can't see. It's only when the doctor says, "I'm sorry, but there is something wrong with the baby's heart, kidneys, or lungs," that happiness is changed to sorrow. This chapter will reveal how one technique—transplantation—is making normal life a possibility for some children.

Attempts at transplantation can be traced to medieval times. Failures then were always attributed to technical problems. Later, in the 1940s, rejection phenomenon was discovered in Oxford, England, by Sir Peter Medawar. He won the Nobel Prize for his discovery, which laid the foundation for the modern era of transplants. In 1967, in South

Africa, the first human heart transplant was performed by Dr. Christiaan Barnard. Dr. Barnard used a technique developed by Dr. Norman Shumway. Since then much progress has been made.

Recent discoveries have renewed hope for thousands of men, women, and children. Just how will be told through the stories of several children.

HEART TRANSPLANT

Baby Laura

Shortly after her birth in June 1984, Laura's parents were told that she had a hole in her heart and serious problems with blood vessels and heart valves. These defects resulted in heart failure, which the doctors had difficulty in treating.

When Laura was just thirteen days old, her doctors inserted a pacemaker into her chest. This electrical device can substitute for a defective natural pacemaker and control the beating of the heart by a series of electrical charges. Over the next six months, however, Laura's condition worsened, and tests showed that her tiny heart couldn't be repaired. Doctors at the University of Michigan Holden Perinatal Hospital were convinced that only a transplant could save her life. But no such operation had ever been successful on anyone so young.

At first, doctors tried to find a local donor in Michigan. This was a slow process, and Laura's condition continued to worsen. Then the day before Thanksgiving, the death of a fourteen-month-old boy in Texas gave hope to Laura's parents. The baby boy was a victim of child abuse, and tests

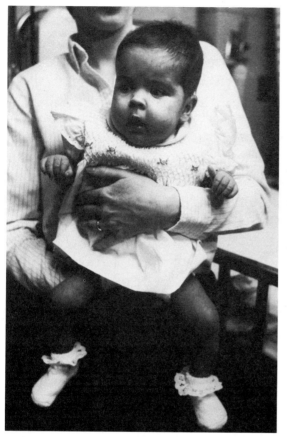

Baby Laura, celebrating her first anniversary of heart transplant on Thanksgiving 1985. She received her heart at five months.

showed no brain activity. Fortunately, his heart was normal and his blood and tissue types were compatible, or in harmony, with Laura's.

Immediately, arrangements were made to charter a small jet and fly a medical team—including a doctor, nurse, anesthetist, and respiratory therapist—to Texas to transport the boy to Michigan. Within hours, they returned. Two teams of physicians worked quickly to prepare both infants for surgery. In a five-hour operation, the boy's heart was implanted in the chest of little Laura. The doctors completed the surgery at 7:30 A.M. on Thanksgiving morning 1984. (A young boy in Michigan received one kidney as well, and the other was sent to Cincinnati. The boy's liver was transplanted into a girl in Kansas City, Missouri.)

There were rough days ahead for Baby Laura. During the critical period after the operation, a mechanical heart outside of Laura's body was successfully used to support the transplanted heart. The doctors were delighted, because, for the first time, they had something to back up the transplanted heart. Historically, transplanted hearts have problems of rejection. The mechanical heart and lungs, developed by Dr. Robert H. Bartlett, gave Laura's own damaged lungs and overburdened heart a chance to rest and heal. Dr. Bartlett's device is small, portable, and can be used for up to two weeks, whereas the standard heart-lung machine has a safe operating time limit of six hours. Dr. Bartlett's device also provides safer control of blood clotting and better control of blood flow.

Rejection of the new organ by the recipient's, or host's, body is always a great possibility. In rejection, the cells of the newly implanted tissue or organ begin to deteriorate because they are rejected by the recipient's immune system. Physicians fight rejection with new drugs like Cyclosporine, or Sandimmune, the breakthrough drug that has recently enabled many major medical centers to resume heart transplants. One week following surgery, Baby Laura had a rejection attack and was given the drug. During the following months, there were other problems, including pneumonia. But, on March 30, 1985, the world's youngest surviving heart transplant was sent home. The eleven-pound, eleven-month-old baby was in good condition. Baby Laura's parents received special instructions regarding her care. They were told to wash their hands before picking her up and to keep her away from crowds and people with infectious illnesses and to wear masks if they have a cold. They also learned about diet and daily medications that Laura will probably have to take for the rest of her life.

On Thanksgiving Day 1985, Baby Laura celebrated her first anniversary of her gift of life. She continues to make progress, and the doctors predict a healthy, normal life for Baby Laura.

Baby Sarah

November 1984 appeared to be a history-making month. Doctors in Houston, Texas, were trying to save another baby with heart problems. Her name is Sarah. Baby Sarah is an active, playful toddler. At twenty months, on November 4, 1985, her mother described her as "just a normal kid." Even so, the memories of her as a critically ill baby still haunt her. Sarah's problems began in July 1984 when she developed a respiratory infection and could barely breathe. Doctors discovered that Sarah had an enlarged heart and that its muscle was rapidly losing its elasticity, which is the ability of the heart to stretch and contract. By September, Sarah was dangerously ill. Her parents were warned that only a transplant would save her. In October, she was put into intensive care to build up her strength for a possible surgical procedure such as a heart transplant.

Baby Sarah, at twenty months in November, 1985. "Just a normal, playful kid," according to her mother. Sarah received her heart transplant when she was eight months old. (The Houston Post.)

Dr. O. Howard Frazier, director of transplantation at Texas Heart Institute, agreed to try a transplant on the baby. The first problem doctors faced was to find a small heart. Other concerns were the unknown impact upon the future growth and development of the baby. On Halloween night, October 31, a two-year-old Dallas girl died of an accidental head injury. Sarah's parents remember that day without difficulty. They faced a dilemma. "It's not a difficult decision when the alternative is death," they say. The next day Sarah received her transplanted heart. Sarah was eight months old.

Now Sarah is growing and gaining weight, and X-rays show that her new heart is growing, too. She is so active that her mother keeps the kitchen chairs turned over on the table, to prevent her from climbing to the salt shaker and sugar bowl. Her three older brothers have learned to keep their bedroom doors closed as protection from roaming Sarah. After a month's hospitalization and three bouts of rejection, this seems miraculous to Sarah's grateful parents.

"Right now, she's living a full life," her mother says. "As for the future, that's the hard part. The doctors don't know what really lies ahead for Sarah." Being first is not always the best position to be in.

Baby Moses

Doctors are watching Baby Moses' progress, too, because he also is a first. Moses, who was a newborn baby at the time, may be the youngest heart transplant patient on record.

Dr. Leonard Bailey, who attempted a radical baboon heart transplant in 1984, performed a rare newborn-to-newborn heart transplant on November 21, 1985, at Loma Linda University Medical Center in California. Baby Moses, the recipient, then four days old, is making excellent progress according to his doctors' report on December 15, 1985.

J. P. Lovett

Because he is older and can communicate and demonstrate his feelings of good health, J.P. caught the media's attention when his surgery was performed in New York in 1984.

Jim and Patricia Lovett of Denver, Colorado, couldn't stop looking for help for their son's damaged heart. When James

P. was born five years earlier, his heart was defective. J.P., as he is affectionately known, was brought to New York for corrective surgery. Unfortunately, J.P. got an infection that damaged his heart muscle. He grew progressively weaker, and doctors feared that he would die. The only possible solution appeared to be a heart transplant. Despite the risk, his parents made the decision.

Later his parents would wonder how long the heart would last—whether it would grow and keep pace with their son's own growth. They worried about their son's psychological development and his ability to fight off the many infections children get. Could little J.P. cope with all of this? J.P. had surgery in June 1984. He was four years old. He received the

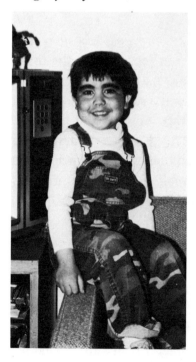

J. P. Lovett at a recent checkup. He received his heart transplant at the age of four. At five-and-a-half he's making excellent progress.

transplant from a child who lived near Columbia Presbyterian Hospital in New York City. He, too, was a young boy who met with an unfortunate accident. The bereaved mother gave the gift to J.P. in memory of her own fun-loving son.

Although J.P. is growing normally and is energetic and lively like children in his age group, there are still years ahead filled with uncertainty. J.P. now rides a tricycle, is learning how to swim, goes camping with his family, and attends school. His parents are cautious but hopeful. The youngster receives monthly supervision from doctors at Columbia Presbyterian Hospital. At specified intervals, doctors extract a tiny piece of J.P.'s heart tissue to look for signs of rejection. This procedure is difficult to perform on small bodies, but J.P. is a brave little patient.

Donna Ashlock

Early in January 1986, a true love story was reported from San Francisco, California. Donna Ashlock, fourteen years old, had a boyfriend who was fifteen. They were very good friends, but Donna had no idea how much Felipe really cared for her. A month earlier, Felipe had told his mother that he had a feeling that something might happen to him—something really bad. If it happened, he said, he wanted Donna to have his heart. Donna had a heart problem, and Felipe wanted her to feel good. So he asked his mom to make sure Donna got his heart. On January 4, 1986, Felipe suddenly became very ill. He died within hours when a blood vessel burst in his brain. Felipe's wish was granted. Donna received her boyfriend's heart. After Donna learned that Felipe's heart was beating in her chest, she realized that Felipe was

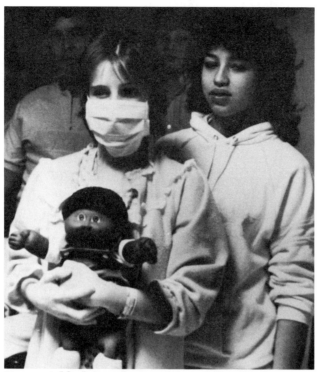

Donna Ashlock hugs her good-luck doll as her best friend cheers her up following her heart transplant from her boyfriend, Felipe.

truly a friend. Donna was discharged from the hospital on January 22, 1986, in good health.

A heart transplant is a living commitment to daily medication, regular trips to the hospital, and possibly an early death. But for now, all of these children are making excellent progress. Despite occasional pain and discomfort, they appear to be happy.

Since the world's first human heart transplant in 1967, more than 260 heart transplants have been performed in the United States. The success rate stands at 70 to 88 percent per year, according to the New York Regional Transplant Program, Inc.

One of the problems potential patients face is the lack of donor hearts. On any given day, more than 1000 people in the New York area alone await transplants of some kind. Sometimes, doctors have to try other means of keeping the patient alive until a heart becomes available. One technique is the use of the artificial heart.

ARTIFICIAL HEART PROGRAM

On October 28, 1985, a federal advisory panel recommended that experiments to implant permanent artificial hearts in a small number of patients be allowed to continue with minor medical and administration changes. So far, mechanical artificial hearts have been implanted permanently in five patients. Three have died and the two others are confined to hospitals, having suffered strokes and other complications. Close supervision by the Food and Drug Administration, which views the data on each patient before permitting the next implant, is one of the recommendations made by the panel. Other changes include such things as recommending the best way to give anticoagulants. Anticoagulants prevent blood clots, which cause strokes, from forming.

Despite some professional criticism and concern regarding artificial hearts, Una L. Clark, widow of Barney Clark, the first recipient, called for "uninterrupted continuation of the program because it is essential to progress."

KIDNEY TRANSPLANT

The history of kidney transplants precedes that of heart transplants. In 1954, the first living related-donor kidney transplant was performed at Boston's Peter Bent Brigham Hospital between identical twins. In 1968, the Uniform Anatomical Gift Act was passed in all fifty states of the country, allowing individuals to donate their organs after death by signing a Uniform Donor Card. In 1973, kidney transplantation increased significantly when the federal government passed a ruling that provided for reimbursement under Medicare for all procedures involved in the acquisition and transplantation of kidneys.

In 1984, over 6000 kidney transplants were performed in the United States. The living related-donor success rate was 85 to 95 percent. Cadaver (transplants from a dead body) donor rate success was 60 to 70 percent.

Dr. Martin Nash is Director of Pediatrics Nephrology at Columbia Presbyterian Hospital in New York. He examines patients and determines the treatment. He explains, "Children go on the dialysis machine when their kidney function deteriorates to the degree that they can no longer get rid of the waste products that have to be eliminated. Dialysis can do this, but not the perfect way that real living kidneys do. In a dialysis treatment, the blood passes through tubes which are constantly bathed by solutions that selectively remove waste materials. Dialysis permits patients to go about their daily activities at work or at school. But with children, as opposed to adults, the dialysis is only a temporary technique. It is a support which allows us time to seek a kidney donor. In other words, children receive dialysis treatments sometimes as long as several years. Then again, a child can be lucky enough to find the right donor in several days."

There are three kinds of dialysis treatments. Of the three kinds, hemodialysis is the most popular. It is the kind mentioned earlier by Dr. Nash and used mostly by his young patients. This technique takes the blood and runs it through a sort of washing machine to take out the impurities and returns it to the body of the patient. Each session lasts about four hours. Patients undergo this "washing" two to three times a week.

Peritoneal dialysis involves putting a tube into the abdominal cavity and forcing fluid into it. With the excess fluid in the cavity, the impurities exit the body. The tube is attached to a bag that receives the fluid.

The choice of method really depends upon the patient's geographical location and the patient. If the patient doesn't live near a large hospital or medical center, he or she will have to do the peritoneal dialysis at home. This means that he or she inserts the tube and drains off the fluids for about forty-five minutes, four times a day. Patients are free to move about, whereas hemodialysis confines them to a bed or chair. In the peritoneal type, the patient and the family are trained by nurses before the patient leaves the hospital on how to maintain strict sterility during the procedure. Infection of the cavity is the biggest problem in doing the procedure at home. If this happens, the parent must call for advice.

The third type of dialysis is Continuous Ambulatory Peritoneal Dialysis (CAPD). This method also uses an implanted peritoneal catheter. Fluid is drained into and from the peritoneal or abdominal cavity by gravity. The patient empties the bag as necessary. This method is considerably less expensive.

Two-thirds of Dr. Nash's pediatric patients are born with some kind of obstruction to the drainage system of their kidneys. The other third undergo dialysis because of disease that they acquired later on during childhood. Both groups are eligible for transplants. Some can receive a kidney from a parent or brother or sister if the donor is older than eighteen. Donors must be adults. If no relatives are available or compatible, then the children must wait for a donor. Many tests are performed to ensure that the child and the donor match. If they do, the kidney must be transplanted no later than seventy-two hours after removal from the donor. Using kidneys from a dead person isn't quite as successful as from a living relative. The body's natural instinct is to reject anything that is foreign. Therefore, donors who are family related and therefore have the most matching genetic characteristics provide the best chance for a successful transplant.

One of Dr. Nash's patients is Sindy, a bright and charming twelve-year-old. She is in the seventh grade when she attends school, which is infrequently. She must spend four hours on the dialysis machine three times a week. Sindy's problems began when she was three years old, and she began dialysis treatments at the age of nine. In November 1984, Sindy received a transplant, but her body rejected it. She is now awaiting another, but meanwhile she seems to spend half of her life on the machine. Despite Sindy's frequent

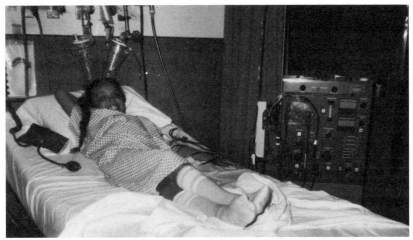

Sindy is on the machine but hopes a kidney will soon be found for her.

absences from school, she is reading at the ninth grade level, enjoys music, her typewriter, and the piano. When there is time, she attends ballet classes. Sindy hopes that she'll get a kidney soon. But for now, this brave and engaging young lady assists the nurses who hook her up to the machine by inserting the needle herself.

Another of Dr. Nash's patients, fourteen-year-old Darlene, received an early Christmas present. Her gift was a kidney, which was transplanted on Thanksgiving Day 1985. The tall, graceful eighth-grader is taking drugs to prevent rejection. Cyclosporine is one of them. She also wears a face mask to protect herself from germs normally found in the air and in contact with people. Darlene's kidney troubles began when she was two. Darlene began taking medication then but had to go on the dialysis machine three months before the transplant. An achiever, Darlene likes science and social

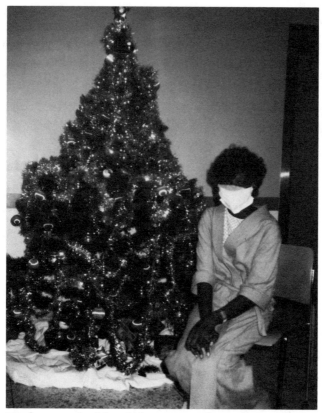

Darlene received her kidney at Presbyterian Hospital on Thanksgiving Day, 1985. She considered it an early Christmas present. She is an eighth grader.

studies. Clinic appointments have caused her to miss school, but her grades are good. Roller skating and riding her bicycle are her favorite ways of relaxing. Darlene prays that her new kidney will function so that she can attend school regularly.

Gary Coleman, teenage star of *Different Strokes* is using a portable dialysis machine. Pint-sized Gary has had kidney problems all of his life. He received his first kidney transplant at the age of five. But, ten years later, the kidney failed. Gary was on dialysis until his second transplant in November 1984. He is being treated for possible rejection. If the kidney must be removed, he will join Sindy in the national computer system that holds the names of those waiting for donors.

The new drug Cyclosporine, public awareness and cooperation, and the Nationwide Computer Network with the United National Organ Sharing (UNOS), which lists those waiting for transplants, are making the wait a little shorter for kids such as Sindy and Gary.

OTHER TRANSPLANTS

Stories of heart, lung, liver, and kidney transplants make the headlines. But doctors across the country are also doing other transplants. The following are some of them.

Pancreas

The first transplant was performed in 1966 by Dr. Lillehei in Minnesota. In 1984, approximately 200 transplants were performed worldwide. The procedure holds promise of "curing" diabetes when technical complications and rejections can be overcome.

Cornea

The cornea is the transparent anterior fibrous coat of the eye. The first transplant was performed in the early 1900s. In 1984, more than 25,000 were done in the United States. The success rate of the operation is 95 percent. Cornea and scleral transplants are used to treat injuries and specific diseases of the eyes. The scleral is the tissue that covers the white of the eye.

Skin

Skin transplants are used to provide temporary cover for victims of severe burns.

Bone Marrow

This transplant is used to treat leukemia and related diseases. The procedure is to destroy the patient's own diseased marrow by irradiation and to replace it with that of a well-matched, living related donor, usually an identical twin or sibling, or identical living related donor.

Bone

Bone can be stored frozen or freeze-dried in sections, chips, slabs, or powdered form. It is used to replace severely injured or cancerous bone.

ORGAN SHORTAGE

The shortage of organs is not due to a lack of potential donors. Enough people die each year under conditions that would allow for the removal of transplantable organs to meet the needs of all potential recipients. The basic problems are the following:

1. The public is not aware of the need for donors or how they can help. In New York, a request is included with every renewal of a driver's license. Few people read it or follow it up.
2. The professional community (doctors and nurses) is not always alert to potential donors; they frequently overlook the possibility of organ donation. Some doctors hesitate to intrude upon a family overcome with grief. Others hesitate because of personal reasons of a religious or ethnic nature.
3. The concept of brain death is difficult to understand. Although thirty-six states have enacted statutes recognizing the determination of death by neurological criteria and six other states have decisions by the highest court clarifying the acceptance of brain death criteria, some physicians and hospitals still express fear of lawsuits and hesitate to participate in organ donation.
4. Some organs, such as hearts and lungs, are more difficult to obtain than others.

The need for organs has increased as the success rate of transplantation continues to improve. Transplantation improves the quality of life; in many cases, it is actually lifesaving.

CHAPTER 5

Finding the Perpetrator

In many ways, medical scientists are like detectives. They seek out the "why" and "what" of disease. They look for clues much like detectives Barnaby Jones and Steve McGarret do. One tool that is vital to both investigators is the laboratory test. While detectives order tests of fingerprints, hair, stains, and shreds of cloth, doctors want technologists to do tests on blood, bone, and tissue. Both hope to get some clues that will lead them to the perpetrator. Like any puzzle, the pieces fit together slowly. For medical scientists—unlike Jones and McGarrett—the puzzle takes longer than sixty minutes.

Without tests, medical sleuths would be severely handicapped. In a hospital, there are many laboratories. Here is a sample of some of them and the tests they perform.

1. The telephone call came during the middle of the night—the time that all bad news seems to arrive. Camp Atwater's nurse told Jody's parents of his 104-degree fever, sore throat, headache, dizziness, and the foul-smelling discharge oozing from his right ear. It is seventy-five miles to the city but only ten miles to a small community hospital. Jody will be taken there to await the arrival of his parents. Meanwhile, the eight-year-old will have a physical examination, and urine and blood tests. To help the pediatrician make a diagnosis, a specimen from Jody's right ear will be sent to the **microbiology** laboratory immediately.

2. It is the bottom of the ninth inning at Shea Stadium in New York City. Forty-two-year-old Al Crawford stands chomping on his fourth hot dog of the afternoon. Between excited gestures and enthusiastic bellows, he gulps down hefty mouthfuls of his favorite brew. The place is in an uproar. It's like the World Series! There are three on and one out! The score is tied four to four! Al's favorite pinchhitter is at the plate. The tension is unbearable. As Al empties the large plastic container, he feels a pain in his chest. Al sits down, because simultaneously he experiences weakness in his legs. The pain squeezes his chest tightly and beads of perspiration explode on his forehead. A friend alerts an usher. In the ambulance, an EMT draws blood for several tests. One test is for levels of Creatine Phospholinase (CPK), an enzyme present in heart muscle. This enzyme increases ten to twenty-five times above the normal level in the first few hours following a heart attack. Upon arrival at Queens Hospital Medical Center, the blood samples will be examined to help the doctor dis-

cover if Al has had a heart attack. The blood samples will be analyzed in the **chemistry** laboratory.

3. "Why don't you clean up your room? Are you going to spend the rest of your life stretched out on that sofa? You haven't touched your dinner!" This scolding expresses the frustration of Tina's mother. Tina's teachers have noticed a decline in interest and achievement in schoolwork, too. Tina's parents insist that she have a physical examination before she can accompany her friends on a weekend skiing trip to Vermont. The doctor will need a complete blood count (CBC) to help him arrive at a decision, since Tina's symptoms are found in so many illnesses. The technician will send the blood sample for examination to a private **hematology** laboratory.

4. While performing her monthly self-examination of her breasts, Myra discovers a tiny lump in the outer portion of her left breast. She is alarmed but comforted by the fact that she can estimate the period of its development. It wasn't there a month earlier. Myra will be examined by a specialist who will perform a biopsy. She may have it down in his office, or she may be required to spend a few hours in a hospital. A sample of the tissue will be surgically removed and examined in a **pathology** laboratory to determine the composition and the kind of treatment recommended, if any.

5. David and Pam have been married for five years. They would love to have children but have been unsuccessful so far. Examination of both of them reveals no specific problem. So, last year, they enrolled in a special program designed to help couples with possible infertility prob-

lems. After several disappointments, they are hopeful and happy. Pam believes that she is pregnant. But, before rushing out to buy a layette, Pam will have a blood specimen taken for an HCG test to make sure that Human Chorionic Gonadotropin hormone is present in her blood. This hormone is present in the blood of a pregnant woman. The blood sample will be sent to the **clinical microscopy** laboratory.

DIAGNOSTIC LABORATORY

Diagnostic laboratories are found in hospitals, private doctors' offices, health care facilities, companies, and private medical firms.

Five types of laboratories were described in the cases you have just read, but there are many more. Over the past ten years, there has been steady progress toward improved accuracy and precision in clinical laboratories. New methods, new instruments, and new quality-control systems have decreased the frequency of laboratory error. "Now most problems are related to communication and interpretation of results. As the volume of tests and data increases, we have more problems," says Dr. Arthur F. Krieg, Director of Clinical Laboratories, Milton S. Hershe Medical Center, Harrisburg, Pennsylvania.

To help with some of these problems, laboratory professionals have used techniques from computer science, management science, and industrial and electrical engineering. These are blended with clinical medicine to establish a first class medical information system. But, a well-designed computer system is at the core of the operation.

Dr. Krieg's prediction of the value of the computer has proved to be valid. Directors of several laboratories share his enthusiasm. One is Laslo Sarkozi, Ph.D., Director of Chemistry Laboratories and professor of Clinical Pathology at Mt. Sinai School of Medicine in New York City. "We received our first laboratory computer system about twelve years ago. We needed it for data handling primarily, because we perform eight thousand to ten thousand tests daily, or three and a half million in a year. Paper work was enormous! Thousands of request slips accumulated in drawers and on desks in nurses' stations. Patients' charts were bulky, and reports could be mislaid and lost easily. The computer provided a clear, legible report and excellent data handling."

Dr. Sarkozi looks forward to the installation of a new computer in 1987. "This one will be large enough to function for all the laboratories like microbiology, nuclear medicine, endocrinology, and others. It will have one hundred and eight terminals, which means that all nursing units will be able to inquire about test results at any time."

A visit to Columbia Presbyterian Hospital provides another response to the use of computers in laboratories. This teaching institution, also in New York City, is concerned with accuracy, too. "Unlike earlier machines that buzzed or flashed when there was a problem, today's machines have extensive error detection systems, which not only tell the operator what the problem is and how to correct it, but also take action themselves," explains Dr. Daniel J. Fink, Director of the Laboratory Information Services. "Some can detect a sample that is too small and instantly alert the technician with a message on the screen. Even more dramatic, if succeeding samples are faulty, the machine can shut down automatically."

Dr. Fink believes that the computer gives the operator a lot of information about the nature of the problem. He says, "The computer keeps on top of the mechanics of each test, from monitoring the temperature of an incubation bath to the intensity of a light bulb, so that the tests are performed under the proper conditions. When something goes wrong, the operator is aware of it immediately. This is yet another assurance that the results are correct."

Most specialists in this field see the introduction of the autoanalyzer—which brought automation by multiple specimen testing—as the most important recent instrument development. Just imagine the following. There are twenty specimen cups filled with blood from patients on an input tray at one time. As the specimen cup on the rotating tray moves into a specific place, an automated arm reaches into the cup, removes a drop of blood, and injects it into a small tube. As air bubbles propel the sample tube along on its winding journey through plastic tubes, chemicals are added. When these chemicals react, the substance that is produced absorbs light at a specific wavelength. At the end of the trip, a light penetrates the changed specimen and a detector measures its power to absorb light. The readings are then converted into simple units. These results are linked to the patients' I.D. numbers. In less than a minute, the computer can provide doctors with a complete profile of the blood chemistry of ten different patients.

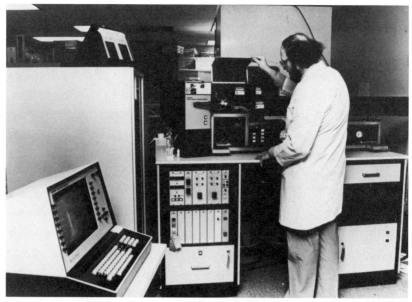

Norman T. Felberg, Ph.D., at Wills checks the laser component of the new cell sorter in his laboratory. The cell sorter counts up to 10,000 cells per minute.

In many of the tests carried out in the laboratory, the computer coordinates each step. Whether it's measuring a sample or mixing precise amounts of chemicals with the sample or timing an incubator period or discarding the sample, the computer runs the show! And computers run it faster and with greater accuracy than ever would be possible without them. At Columbia Presbyterian Hospital in the precomputer days, only about sixty profiles an hour were processed. Today, it is possible to do one hundred in half the time. The computers have shortened the waiting time for results from a day to a couple of hours.

Computers can help the physician in prescribing drug dosage, too. For example, before the physician can match an antibiotic to the offending microorganism, the physician must know to which medication the "bug" is sensitive, where the infection is in the body, and how sensitive that area is to the antibiotic. Because the computer specializes in storing lots of information, it plays the mix-and-match game and tells the doctor how effective each of the tested drugs might be. Then the doctor selects the best drug for the job.

A third site, Cornell Medical Center New York Hospital, provides another view of usefulness of the computer. Before computerization, communication was minimal, since laboratories are scattered from the twenty-second floor to the basement of the 1100-bed teaching hospital. To get laboratory

SMAC II in the chemistry laboratory at Presbyterian Hospital, New York City.

results, a physician had to call individual laboratories. Specimens were frequently lost and duplication was common. But Dr. Marvin Tessler, the laboratory manager, says, "Now computerized Audit-trail, which is a tracking system, permits us to track a specimen through the system. We can discover if it physically arrived at the laboratory, and if testing is in progress. Physicians call one telephone number and get results of all tests requested."

All three directors were asked how the computer has affected the technologist. Dr. Sarkozi responded, "Formerly, the operator set dials and wheels and often had to plot the test results on a graph by hand. Now the operator makes adjustments by pushing a button on a keyboard and the computer displays a graph on the screen." Dr. Fink adds, "The computer has created more dialogue between the operator and the machine. And the computers check the operators, too." Dr. Tessler's appraisal: "Accuracy and speed were the goals determined for the computer. This is being done and the technologists enjoy their work even more."

Ms. Dorothy Eng agrees with Dr. Tessler. She is a technologist at New York Hospital and has the responsibility of training computer users in the blood bank. "The initial reaction to the laboratory computer was fear that it would replace staff, especially clerical staff. But in fact, this hasn't happened. Before the computer, we would get a lot of calls asking us if blood was ready for transfusions. Now these routine questions are answered by the Communications Center. When the system is down several hours for monthly maintenance, the floors call us. During this period, it amuses me to hear comments like 'How did we ever do without a computer?'"

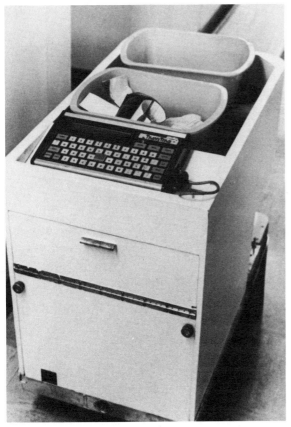

Clancy, a computerized battery-powered robot collects and delivers specimens for the labs at Yale New Haven Hospital.

Technicians and technologists may not be replaced, but messengers should be on the lookout for "Clancy." Clancy is a $1000 robot at the Yale New Haven Hospital. He collects the specimens sent to the hospital's laboratories and delivers them to the appropriate work stations. Clancy, a computerized, battery-powered white cart, follows a pattern of tapes laid on the floor. The robot is doing a super job, according to hospital officials. It completes in ten minutes what before took five messengers about two hours to do, and in twenty months of round-the-clock operation has never broken down. The robot announces its arrival with a beep and goes on to its next stop when its "go" button is pushed. Clancy was created by the hospital engineering staff and others. They are now working on another robot that will be able to climb stairs or use the elevator to enlarge the area of operation.

BLOOD BANK

One of the most important laboratory services in any hospital is the blood bank. Unless you, a relative, or a friend has required a life-sustaining transfusion, this laboratory may be totally unfamiliar to you. Although every hospital has a blood bank, there are large blood distribution centers that provide services to the general public. The New York Blood Center has a highly automated system that links every blood donor through transfusions made from blood donations. Eric Brodheim, Ph.D., Vice-President of Systems, Planning, and Operations at the center, describes the operation: "The system involves the Blood Center, hospitals which receive blood from the center, and hemophiliac care centers which use blood parts. When a donor gives blood, that blood is separated into as many as five transfusable parts with unique identifying numbers of the donation. Blood samples are drawn for determination of blood groups and Rhesus, or RH, types. Screening for antibodies which may cause transfusion problems, hepatitis, or other possible transmitted blood diseases is completed, too. All of this information must be made available quickly, because leukocytes, (white blood cells), must be transfused within six hours of collection. Accuracy is vital, because a misclassification can possibly mean death to the recipient getting an incompatible blood type."

The computer is vital to the operations of the center. Each step in the handling of a blood donation is done in a different laboratory by a variety of technicians. The information is fed into the computer, which links all the steps and determines their accuracy through repeated tests.

Machine-readable codes are placed on blood packages to be distributed to 240 hospitals in several states. These codes are similar to those that appear on grocery store items in supermarkets, which the checkout clerk scans with a scanner. The scanner, in this instance, identifies what parts are being shipped and their hospital destination. The receiving hospitals are automated, too, and, in turn, scan the blood before it goes into their blood banks, making it part of their own inventories. The New York Blood Center operates five blood centers and services the entire metropolitan area. This means it services about 20 million people. "It is a large operation," says Dr. Brodheim. "We collect about six hundred thousand units of blood each year, which is two thousand units a day. And out of this, we make transfusable blood parts. This creates a great deal of work for the computer."

The center operates a reference laboratory. When people have difficulty in matching because of unique characteristics in their blood, their blood samples are sent to the center. These samples are analyzed with care to determine the source of difficulty. "From our supply of rare bloods, we find a compatible sample."

The computer often plays detective, too. If someone develops hepatitis following a transfusion, a search is conducted to find the culprit because there is a risk that hepatitis is transmitted through blood transfusion. "We may go back six months or even a year to learn the identity of the donors of the products that were transmitted to the patient. We also want to learn more about the disposition of that particular blood. What else was made from the blood? Where were they sent? Who received them? These areas of investigation continue to have priority. It's important to locate all persons involved cautiously and quickly," Dr. Brodheim states.

Recently, the center has been engaged along with other research institutions in the investigation of AIDS. Because of the possibility that the disease is one that is transmitted through transfusions, the center has been working with local health officials and the National Center for Disease Control in Atlanta, Georgia.

At least three to four requests are received at the center each day from people engaged in a worldwide search for unusual blood. "Ninety-nine percent of the time, people needing blood can be transfused with compatible blood. But one percent of cases have unusual components which require a worldwide search. First, we must discover what is compatible and then find the units. This center has one of the largest 'stores' of frozen rare blood in the world. It may become a global search, because if we don't have it, we call upon our associations," says Dr. Brodheim with pride.

The Manhattan Blood Center makes a special effort to care for the needs of sickle cell and Cooley's anemia patients. Another group—hemophiliacs—need a great deal of blood, too. There are 20,000 hemophiliacs in the entire country. This group alone could use the clotting factor from every pint of blood collected in the United States. Sickle cell anemia,

Cooley's disease, and hemophilia affect children. At one time, few afflicted children would have reached maturity or even eighteen years of age. Now, most can expect to live a normal life span because of new approaches to treatment.

Sickle Cell Anemia

It is the beginning of the school year. The school doctor is having a meeting with all the new teachers at Acorn Elementary School. Because Acorn has a large population of minority children, Dr. Petrie will also talk about a chronic disease called sickle cell anemia.

The first doctor in America to report the disease was Dr. J. B. Herrick. He first came across this extraordinary condition in 1910 while examining a black student. Sickle cell anemia is a condition in which there is an abnormality of the hemoglobin of the red blood cells. Hemoglobin is the iron-containing pigment of red blood cells that carries oxygen to all parts of the body. Normal red blood cells have a round shape like a doughnut, but sickle cells are banana-shaped, crescent, or sickled in shape. In the United States, about one in every twelve black people has the trait, while one out of every 500 black people is afflicted with the anemia. Other groups that may have the disease include Greeks, Italians, Arabs, Asiatic Indians, and Turks.

Dr. Petrie tells the new teachers that sickle cell anemia is inherited and that the genes for the disease must be present at birth for the child to be affected. For a child to have sickle cell anemia, he or she must have a pair of these genes—one from the mother and one from the father. This means that both parents have the gene for sickle cell hemoglobin. If only one parent has the gene, the child will only have the sickle cell trait. A child with the trait is not considered ill but is a carrier of the gene. The disease is not contagious.

The teachers are told to follow up any youngster who has frequent absences from school or who is thin and small for his or her age. When not having pain, the child may be as active as any other child but is likely to tire easily. There are periods when the disease is more active. These times are called crises, and they are often brought on by colds and other childhood infections.

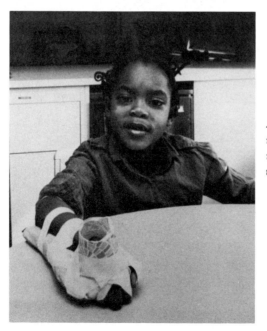

A sickle cell anemia victim manages a smile while receiving treatment during a crisis attack.

Fortunately, the disease tends to become milder as the child grows into adolescence and adulthood. Crises are less often and less severe. There is no specific treatment.

Regular transfusions prevent painful crises and are sometimes used. But if patients have frequent transfusions, they may get too much iron in their bodies. (Iron is found in red blood cells.) To prevent this, patients who need transfusions are given a special new drug now that prevents this iron overload. Another problem with transfusions is that in many parts of the country it is difficult to find blood that is properly typed. Giving children the wrong type of blood can cause them to develop many more antibodies to red blood cell transfusions, so many clinics now only transfuse if children are in real crisis and blood cells are breaking down. Some children on chronic transfusion have had strokes. Strokes can occur early in sickle cell anemia. When necessary, there are alternative drugs that can be given to prevent this from happening.

With the exception of strenuous sports, a child with the disease may carry on the usual activities of his or her peer group. Progress has been made in recognizing the disease and treating it. Affected children can develop like other children. Their parents need help first in learning how to cope and adjust to the disease and then in transferring these attitudes to their children.

New research that is being carried out at Boston's Beth Israel Hospital appears to be effective. Researchers have designed three techniques to reduce the sickling of red cells which causes the painful crises. The objective is to affect change in the red blood cells and to treat the patient before rather than after the problem arises. Low-salt diet is being tried in another study in an attempt to prolong the life span of red blood cells in patients. Normally, red blood cells live 120 days. In sickle cell anemia patients, their life span is only fifteen to twenty days. Proposed drug therapy promises to reduce the number of crises by increasing the number of red blood cells.

Dr. Robert Rosa of Harvard Medical School, director of this research, says the traditional treatment of oxygen, drugs, and blood transfusions has not produced consistent beneficial effects. "And many patients are desperate for help. They are frustrated because one day they're well and the next day, they're in the hospital. If one of our new therapies or a combination of several should prove successful, we might substantially improve the lives of these patients."

In addition to the research, schools and departments of health frequently hold health fairs where they offer free testing for the trait. In some communities, this testing is automatically part of every child's examination. The test is simple, quick, and painless. In New York State, every new mother may have her baby tested before she brings the child home from the hospital. A small amount of blood, taken from the baby's heel, is examined at a New York State public health laboratory for signs of any genetic disease.

Finally, to help parents understand the disease, there are support groups, or parents' clubs. These groups have formed in large cities around the country. They serve as a means of information and provide a forum in which parents can discuss common problems in a constructive way.

Hemophilia

Hemophilia is another hereditary blood disorder, but unlike the others, it mainly affects male children. Although most of the time it is inherited, hemophilia can occur in families without a known history of the disease.

Hemophilia is caused by the inactivity of one of the blood proteins necessary for clotting. This means that once a hemophiliac starts to bleed, the blood fails to clot and abnormal bleeding occurs. The disease is classified as mild, moderate, or severe, depending upon the percentage of active clotting factors in the blood. People with severe hemophilia have less than one percent of the normal levels of active clotting factor present in the blood.

Sons usually have the condition passed to them by their mothers, who usually are not hemophiliacs themselves but are carriers and have normal clotting ability. In most families, there is a history of the disease, but up to a third of newly diagnosed cases may be without a history. Daughters may carry the gene but rarely have symptoms of the disease. A hemophiliac male cannot pass the disease on to his sons, but he can pass the hemophilia gene to his daughters who, although they are unlikely to have the disease, will have the potential to pass hemophilia on to succeeding generations.

There are at least 20,000 males in the United States who have the disease. Since it occurs in one out of every 4000 live male births, this population is expected to continue to grow. Medical advances have enabled the hemophiliac to approach a normal life expectancy. Many people think hemophiliacs bleed faster then other people, but this is not true. Dr. Margaret Hilgarten, Chief of the Department of Pediatric Hematology at New York Hospital Medical Center, explains, "To the contrary, hemophiliacs do not bleed faster but may bleed for a longer period of time. They do not bleed to death either from minor external wounds. The main problem for the hemophiliac is uncontrolled internal bleeding, which can come on without any reason. Over a period of time, bleeding into joints and muscles can cause permanent damage and chronic pain."

Years ago, hemophiliacs received whole blood transfusions, but now they receive a clotting factor developed from human blood. This factor stays in the patients' bloodstreams for a while. Every time internal bleeding occurs, additional clotting factors are needed. Although these are excellent ways of controlling the disease, there is no cure for hemophilia. A child born with the disease will have it throughout his life.

Treatment has dramatically changed the quality of life for the hemophiliac and his family. The availability of plasma clotting factors in concentrated form has made the difference. Says Dr. Hilgarten: "This permitted us to begin a Home Care Program. We teach families how to give the factor to young children. The older ones, ages ten and up, are taught how to infuse themselves at home when they bleed. Then these youngsters are not dependent upon family or the hospital. This means that families can travel, children can go to school away from home, go to camp, and visit relatives. They can be quite independent and only need to come to the hospital for their biannual, or twice a year, examination. At that time, we

A young hemophiliac prepares to infuse himself with a clotting factor, made from human blood, which remains active in his blood for a short period of time. Some youngsters do so well that they only need the factor several times a month.

check to see that they are responding to the factor the way they should, if they are assuming responsibility, and determine if there has been any bleeding in the joints. This is where most hemophiliacs bleed, and unnoticed, it can cause a problem."

In hemophiliacs, notice of excess bleeding begins with circumcision or when they are learning to walk alone and have frequent falls. Bleeding is for life, unfortunately. Internal bleeding is critical. Children bleed as a result of hard falls, but they bleed from soft falls, too. Examples of soft falls might

John Apicella at work in the family's jewelry business. John Jr. lives a normal life despite his hemophilia. He enjoys active, contact sports, too.

be bumping against a piece of furniture or a person. If the bump involves a previously injured joint, this light bump can cause internal bleeding.

Youngsters must avoid contact sports like football, basketball, and soccer. If their joints are in good condition, they can enjoy bowling, golf, tennis, and swimming. Hemophiliacs must receive their medical supervision at a federally funded regional center. Although the condition is rare, it is lifelong and included in the classification of chronic illnesses for which the government supplies expertise, or the specialists who know how to treat the victim and his family.

Many of the victims can now look forward to a normal life. John Apicella is one. John is eighteen now and works in his family's jewelry business. He graduated from La Salle High School in good standing, but, for the moment, he is not planning on college. John has been administering factors to himself since the age of ten. He only does it once a month. He is also very active and enjoys sports such as basketball, football, baseball, and soccer. He says that he has always been careful and avoids roughhouse tactics to protect himself. He has two brothers and one sister, but he is the only one with hemophilia.

Thalassemia, or Cooley's Disease

Thalassemia is the Greek name, but most people know this disease by its Italian name—Cooley's disease. With this anemia, progress has been much slower. Children with this anemia require chronic blood transfusions, because they cannot make the proper type of hemoglobin. Hemoglobin carries oxygen from the lungs to the tissues of the body. In Cooley's anemia the red blood cells are broken down rapidly, making it necessary to replace them through transfusions regularly. When these patients—like the sickle cell anemia patients—receive too much iron, which the body cannot use or get rid of, the patients die of iron toxicity rather than the Cooley's anemia.

Dr. Hilgarten talks about a new drug that is helping children: "Over the past ten years, we have developed a drug that binds the iron and helps the body to excrete, or get rid of, it in the urine and the stool. But parents must give the children the drug every day. This is a problem, because the drug is given in rather large doses. It is also given under the skin by an automatic pump. The pump is put in place before the child goes to bed and the pump works during sleep, administering the drug. If this is too difficult for the parents, the child must be admitted to the hospital twice a month for the treatment. It seems to be working. The children are not having symptoms of iron toxicity until much later. So many more of the patients are living until ages twenty and thirty. Children with sickle cell anemia are using the new drug, too, since they too require transfusion when in crisis and are apt to get iron overload."

Intensive parent education needs to be stressed now. New drugs are prolonging life, but parents and children need to be more aware of what the gift of life means and how to cope with a chronic illness.

CHAPTER 6

Improving the Quality of Life

Days lost from school. . . . Days lost from work. . . . Days lost from play. . . . Millions of days lost from picnics, hiking, camping, vacations, and sports events all because of chronic illnesses. Many happy and not so happy days lost because of asthma attacks, allergies, lung congestion, headache, joint pains, dizzy spells, and many more ailments that keep so many people from living a full life. This chapter will review some of those chronic diseases that are being better understood by using knowledge from recent research combined with new tools. The result is hope for a better life for millions of children and adults.

ASTHMA

At the Elm Street Junior High School, Mr. Peters looks at the attendance records of his twenty-five pupils. It is January, and a bitter cold wind rattles the windowpanes in the old school building. Neither Mark, Jennifer, nor Keith will be in today, he says to himself. Sara and Danny had runny noses yesterday, so Mr. Peters does not expect them either. Then there is Katie, whose mother had a new baby recently. Katie will be absent, too.

How does Mr. Peters know all of this? He knows because all six children have asthma. Attacks can be triggered, among other things, by weather, infections, and emotional upsets. Asthma, a year-round condition, causes children to miss more school days and adults to miss more work days than the common cold. Of the six million Americans estimated to have asthma, 2.1 million are children. It is the most common chronic disease of childhood.

Asthma is not new. It has been described in the ancient medical literature of most cultures. The word "asthma" comes from the ancient Greek word *aenai,* which means to blow or pant. The disease affects people of all ages, races, and socioeconomic levels.

Asthma constricts the air tubes in the lungs as if one were squeezing a garden hose and halting the flow of water. The patient with asthma feels tightness in the chest; he or she coughs, wheezes, and has great difficulty in breathing. For many hospitals, asthma is the leading cause of acute hospitalization in children.

For patient and family, an asthmatic attack can be a frightening experience. Since an attack can come on suddenly, there are many false stories about asthma, which many people believe. The following is a list of some of the myths that Dr. Jonathan Weiss, of Cornell Medical Center, New York Hospital's Department of Psychiatry, has heard:

1. Asthma is in the patient's head.
2. It's really a psychological problem.
3. If they want to, children can turn asthma on and off.
4. Children develop asthma because of their personalities.

All of these statements are false. Asthma is a physical not a psychological disease. It starts in the body, not the mind. As often as not, the emotional problems that asthmatic children have are the result, rather than the cause, of their illness. For example, it used to be thought that asthmatic children held onto their feelings too tightly and didn't cry like "normal" children. Wheezing was believed to be a strangled cry. Now, however, it's been suggested that asthmatic children try not to cry, because they've learned that crying can trigger asthma episodes. Shyness, dependency, and other personality styles that characterize some asthmatic children are probably also the result of their illness.

One of the ways asthmatics are helping themselves today is by using relaxation techniques. These can be practiced almost anywhere. Janice has had asthma most of her eleven years of life. She has learned how to help herself to ward off an attack. "I get very tense just before a test. I perspire and begin to shake. Geometry is one of my best subjects and I like it. But when there is a test, I find myself breathing faster, because I'm nervous. I've learned to close my eyes, put my hands palms down on my knees, and lower my head. I start with my feet and work up to my shoulders in just 'letting go.' I get as limp as possible and sit quietly for two or three minutes before starting the test."

In addition to relaxation techniques, asthmatics are helped by breathing exercises done with or without machines. Deep

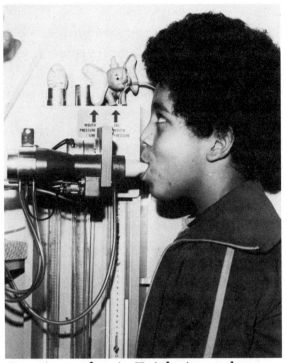

Roger is an asthmatic. He is having a pulmonary function test to see if he is getting enough oxygen into his lungs.

breathing can be learned and may prevent an attack. Yoga or karate encourage breath control, self-discipline, and body awareness in addition to providing physical exercise without prolonged running. Swimming and gymnastics are also good for asthmatics.

Research departments of major universities and hospitals are now working to find new solutions to this old problem. Experts and scientists from all over the country are studying, testing, and researching the role that viruses play in asthma, how to control allergic reactions, how heredity affects asthma, why some patients get severe episodes that dramatically emerge hours after the initial symptoms appear, and much more. Research is bringing new and better ways of preventing and treating asthma. The future is bright.

CYSTIC FIBROSIS

Giselle is twelve years old. Every afternoon after school, she has a lesson or activity of some sort. On Monday, it's tennis. On Tuesday, Giselle has a date with her violin and Professor Zeigler. Wednesday, she is a candy striper learning how to be a volunteer aide. It's swimming on Thursday. But Friday is the day for her favorite lesson, which is ballet. This weekly schedule seems heavy enough, yet Giselle must add another four hours a day in treatment for cystic fibrosis!

Giselle is one of the 32,000 young people in the United States with cystic fibrosis, the most common life-threatening genetic disease affecting young people. Cystic fibrosis affects even more young people than sickle cell anemia. Years ago, few of its victims had a future. But it is no longer the automatic child-killer that it once was.

It is believed that about ten million Americans unknowingly carry the gene for cystic fibrosis. If two such people marry, their children may inherit the disease. The clinical effects of cystic fibrosis may become apparent soon after birth or they may take several years to develop. Symptoms can include a distended or large abdomen, vomiting, dehydration or low levels of body fluids, and pale-looking stools due to the baby's inability to absorb fats. Older children show slow weight gain in spite of excessive appetites, have sallow-looking skin, thin arms and legs, and perspire excessively. Patients also have recurrent attacks of bronchitis and pneumonia. Treatment includes drugs and vitamins, a low-fat diet with generous salting of food, breathing exercises, chest physical therapy to loosen mucus plugs, and postural drainage. Postural drainage means hanging the trunk of the body over the side of the bed to remove excess secretions from the respiratory track. Respiratory complications cause 90 percent of the deaths among the victims.

In 1966, fewer than 6 percent of children with the disease lived beyond the age of fifteen. Today, children born with the disease have a fifty-fifty chance of reaching the age of twenty-one. In fact, their chances of growing up to graduate from college and marry are quite good. An example is Dr. John Z. Jacoby III.

Dr. Jacoby is one of the few physicians in the country who really knows the physical and mental torment of this illness as well as the victims he treats. Dr. Jacoby not only has fought his own battle with cystic fibrosis since the age of four, but he also saw his younger sister die from it in 1970.

Dr. Jack, as his patients call him, directs the cystic fibrosis clinic and services at St. Vincent's Hospital in New York City, which serves 1500 outpatients each year. Like his patients, he undergoes four hours of therapy every day. In addition to an enriched diet and antibiotics, he has chest physical therapy. The therapist pounds on Dr. Jack's back, which helps to loosen the heavy mucus that blocks the lungs and bronchial tubes. He also drinks lots of water to keep respiratory secretions as loose as possible.

Researchers are excited by recent genetic discoveries that could revolutionize detection, prevention, and correction of cystic fibrosis. In October 1985, several research teams from the United States, Canada, and England announced that they had located the cystic fibrosis gene in the large amount of material in the cell's genetic matter. They discovered linkages between the cystic fibrosis gene and other known genes, which could help them identify the presence of the cystic fibrosis gene. The next steps are to eliminate or limit its effect upon the body. Scientists believe that the happy day may not be too far away.

MENTAL ILLNESS IN CHILDREN AND ADOLESCENTS

Julio is nine years old, but he hasn't attended school for more than a year. He was suspended for setting fires in the supply closets of his classroom. Debby is only twelve, but she has a long history of running away from home. She steals money from her family, friends, and others. George is six feet tall and thirteen years old. He beat up everyone in his sixth grade class, including his teacher.

All of these children are in mental hospitals receiving medical and psychiatric treatment, which will help them eventually to return to their families and friends. One new instrument being used in their treatment program is the computer. Instead of the restless, jittery, and angry behavior the children showed on admission to the hospital, they now sit quietly in front of computers. In one hospital—Metropolitan Medical Center in New York—children like Julio, Debby, and George spend hours every day practicing math problems, following reading exercises, writing letters, and playing games together. They have become computer whizzes! A year has passed since the patients began to learn how to use the computer. In that time, doctors, teachers, and learning disability specialists at the hospital improved the academic and communication skills of the patients.

Dr. Mark Lepper, a professor of psychology at Stanford University, believes that the computer provides the right level of success, mastery, and control for the children, and enables them to approach subjects that in the past meant failure for them.

The thirty patients in the children's psychiatric ward at Metropolitan are accustomed to failure in their contact with other people. Their disturbances range from conduct disorders to schizophrenia, and many have been in hospitals for years. Dr. Leonard Davidman, the chief psychologist in the children's and adolescents' ward at Metropolitan, attributes the success of the computer to its ability to give individual treatment to patients who are easily frustrated. Individual attention always helps. Dr. Davidman explains: "We can't have one thousand staff members there. This computer talks to them."

Children with abnormally short attention spans concentrate in front of the computer for more than an hour at a time. Others who before had trouble relating to their peers are now able to play with them regularly. Some with learning disabilities who used to be afraid of tests or even simple reading and writing tasks now volunteer to practice on the educational computer programs.

Dr. Leonard Davidman, child psychologist, helps a patient tell the computer his thoughts.

Another bonus Dr. Davidman sees is that the computer gives the patients a chance to express what they learn in therapy without the conflict that they might experience when a therapist is present. As one patient put it, "I could never say anything nice without the computer. When you get real mad and you get angry, you can't tell that to a person, because it winds up in physical violence. But you can even curse on the computer."

The individualized approach is most important for these children. Dr. Davidman believes that the most crucial struggle for institutionalized children is keeping up with mainstream youth in some way. The number one goal is giving kids what they'd normally have if they were not locked away. The computer seems to be helping.

CHILDHOOD CANCERS

After weeks of doctors' examinations and tests, Gweneth and her parents were on their way to Memorial Sloan-Kettering Center in New York. The ten-month baby was restless as her parents tried to comfort her within the limited space provided by two airplane coach seats. Cabin attendants were helpful, but the more than three hour ride from Phoenix, Arizona, had been hard on the ill baby. Learning their baby had cancer was shocking news to the young parents, who were just beginning to enjoy their beautiful first child. Leaving home and family to go and live in New York for several months caused additional stress. Thoughts of medical bills, living costs, and loss of income aggravated an already tense situation.

Several years ago, these problems would have determined whether or not a child received excellent medical care. But today, people like Gweneth and her parents can look forward to a lot of support. First, many children with cancer are being cured. Second, there is the Ronald McDonald House, a home away from home.

Cancer is second only to accidents as the leading cause of death among children in the United States. The number of children under the age of 15 who get cancer is 12 out of every 100,000 white children and 9 out of every 100,000 black children. More than 40 percent of childhood cancers occur in the very young; that is, ages 4 and younger.

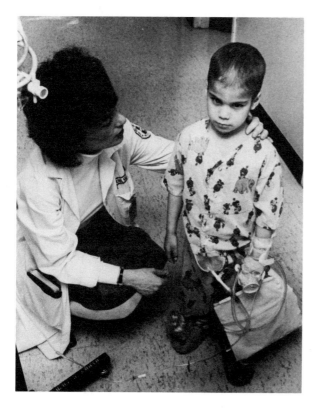

Social worker Naomi Schrenzel chats with three-year-old pediatric cancer patient strolling along a corridor at Babies Hospital.

The four major childhood cancers in this country are acute leukemia (lymphomas, or cancer of the lymph system), neuroblastoma (a cancer in one type of immature nerve cell), Wilms' tumor (cancer of the kidney), and retinoblastoma (an eye cancer). Of these four types of cancer, leukemia is the most common.

The word *leukemia* means "white blood." It was first given to the disease by the German pathologist Virchow in 1847. Leukemia is a cancer of the lymph nodes or bone marrow, which make the blood cells. It occurs not only in humans but also in animals such as cattle, mice, guinea pigs, and cats. If leukemia affects a young person quickly, it is called "acute" because it comes on suddenly and progresses rapidly in the absence of treatment.

Acute Lymphocytic Leukemia, or ALL, is known as childhood leukemia. It is the most commonly occurring cancer in childhood. It affects the lymphocytes, which are the white blood cells. Most children are between two and eight years old when diagnosed, but the disease can occur in people in their twenties and thirties as well. For reasons still not understood, ALL affects more boys than girls and occurs more frequently among white children than black children.

ALL is treated with radiation and various combinations of drugs, or chemotherapy. Currently, there are more than thirty drugs that can be used to control leukemia in both children and adults.

Just fifteen years ago, the average life expectancy for children with leukemia was only one year. Remissions (the temporary or long-term return to good health) were obtained in only 25 percent of those early victims. Now, better diagnosis, new combinations of drugs, radiation treatment, and bone marrow transplants have caused a dramatic reversal of those statistics. Today, 90 percent of young victims of the most common childhood leukemia go into remission, and over half of those children appear to be cured.

Bone marrow transplants have extended lives for many leukemia patients. Some appear completely cured. At present, the transplant approach is possible only in patients for whom a type-matched donor—usually a family member—can be found. A parent or sibling would naturally have the nearest similarity in bone marrow composition.

The progress in the control and understanding of leukemia has been rapid over the past fifteen years. The final cure for leukemia will come from research into the understanding of its causes, into the nature of the defects that keep cells from developing normally, and into methods for controlling the leukemia white cells. Also needed are better procedures for supportive therapy to avoid the serious complications of leukemia and better treatments, such as bone marrow transplants.

Part of the supportive therapy for childhood cancer is a network of Ronald McDonald Houses, which provide much needed overnight housing for families. Across the country, there are twenty of these houses in such places as Atlanta, Boston, Philadelphia, Chicago, Cleveland, Pittsburgh, Minneapolis, and New York. The first house opened in Philadelphia in 1974 when a Philadelphia Eagles football player, Fred Hill, enlisted the aid of the local McDonald's restaurant and others in the project. Mr. Hill's seven-year-old daughter had leukemia, and the family needed accommodations close to the hospital where she was being treated.

New York has the largest facility with twenty bedrooms, as well as seven public rooms where people can gather. These include an elegant living room, a library, a basement playroom, and a large airy kitchen with two large dining rooms. In New York, the cost per night is six dollars. In hardship cases, even this may be waived. The house is run by the Children's Oncology Society of New York. It is located within reach of the city's major hospitals, although most children are treated at Memorial. Of the 6000 children diagnosed each year as having cancer, 600 live in the metropolitan New York area and another 300 come to New York for treatment from outside the tristate area.

The goal of the house is to allow for shared emotions and feelings. It is through shared experiences that families get hope, strength, and practical assistance in learning how to cope with their child's illness. The philosophy of shared experience is perhaps best shown in the playroom and kitchen of McDonald House. The large, cheerfully decorated basement playroom offers a variety of entertainment options, from board games to pinball, puppets, and blocks. There is a color television, easels for painting, and a children's library. It is a place where both teenagers and younger children can find something to do.

A NEW APPROACH TO CANCER TREATMENT

National Cancer Institute (NCI) scientists have developed a new approach to cancer treatment that successfully activates the immune system to destroy cancer cells in patients whose cancers are so far advanced that they no longer respond to chemotherapy or radiation. This research team, led by Steven A. Rosenberg, M.D., Ph.D., chief of the surgery branch in NCI's Division of Cancer Treatment, reported findings in the December 5, 1985, *New England Journal of Medicine*.

The scientists use specialized machines to remove circulating white blood cells, known as lymphocytes, from the patients. The critical part of this technique is the treatment of these lymphocytes with an immune system activator, or lymphokine, called Interleukin-2 (IL-2). IL-2 converts the lymphocytes into lymphokins activated killer (LAK) cells that are capable of destroying cancer cells but not normal cells.

The scientists infuse these LAK cells with IL-2, back into the patient. The IL-2 induces the LAK cells to multiply for a short time in the body, thus enhancing their ability to destroy cancer cells.

Among twenty-five patients with advanced cancers treated with this new approach to immunotherapy, the researchers found that eleven patients, or 44 percent, had measurable tumor reductions of at least 50 percent. These responses occurred in patients with melanoma, colorectal, kidney, and lung cancers.

Dr. Rosenberg's team hopes to improve the technique and plans future studies. "This treatment approach is still in a developmental stage, and considerable refinement is necessary before its role in cancer therapy can be definitively established," he says.

HEART DISEASE

More people in the United States die of coronary heart disease than from any other illness. This kind of heart trouble damages the coronary arteries which nourish the heart muscle. By the age of sixty, every fifth man and one in seventeen women have some form of heart disease. One out of every fifteen men and women will eventually have a stroke. Heart disease caused by fat-clogged arteries will claim many victims, too.

The Framingham Heart Study, completed by Dr. W. P. Castelli and reported in the February 1984 *American Journal of Medicine,* identified several factors that contribute to an increased risk of heart attacks and strokes. Doctors are able to predict potential victims years before they become ill. However, it can be shown that the risk of heart and cardiovascular disease can be reduced.

1. *Do not smoke.* Smokers have more than twice the risk of heart attacks as nonsmokers. The earlier a person starts smoking, the higher the risk. When smokers stop smoking, the risk goes down.
2. *Eat a nutritious diet* that is low in cholesterol and fats. This diet avoids heart-damaging foods such as saturated, or hard, animal fats found in butter, lard, and egg yolk. Recommended are meals using grains, fruits, vegetables, lean meats, chicken, and fish.
3. *Hypertension* or high blood pressure plus a diet high in fats and cholesterol can add up to serious trouble. Some sixty million Americans have high blood pressure. Many of these people are unaware of its presence, since it doesn't cause obvious symptoms. Because it tends to run in families, even babies as young as six months are susceptible. Campaigns to make the public aware of this silent killer are underway in the United States. It can be managed if discovered early. Limited salt intake, exercise, and drugs are part of the treatment. New and better drugs are being discovered all the time.
4. *Obesity,* or being overweight, particularly starting as a child or gaining weight in later years is associated with

hypertension. Wise eating habits started early in life can set a pattern for life. "Less is better" is a good rule to follow.

5. *Tension and stresses* in the various ways we live are known to have a bad effect on our health. Some people can cope with fear, anxiety, and challenge; others cannot. Employee assistance programs that help employees find solutions to problems of all kinds provide some relief. Shorter work weeks, frequent minivacations, support groups, child care, and mental health services all help reduce stress. Exercise has merit. Taking long walks; swimming; playing tennis, handball, or basketball; or riding a bicycle are beneficial. There is no magic in specific, rigid exercise programs which are frequently boring. Conditioning is helpful because the heart gets accustomed to being put under some kind of stress. Regular exercise also makes you feel better, helps to burn up some calories, and may help to reduce the levels of fat in the bloodstream.

The most benefit is expected to come from the growing trend of teaching young children how to be responsible for their own health. Children today must be made aware of the harmful effects of smoking, lack of exercise, being overweight, and eating greasy, fatty foods.

DIABETES

Diabetes is the name for a group of chronic, or lifelong, diseases that can be controlled but as yet not cured. It affects the way the body uses food. Diabetes develops either because the body does not produce enough insulin or because what is produced cannot be used effectively by the body cells. There are two types of diabetes.

Type I, which was formerly called juvenile diabetes, occurs most often in children and young adults. It accounts for about 10 percent of all cases of diabetes. Because the pancreas (one of the endocrine glands) produces little or no insulin, these patients must take daily injections to stay alive.

Type II usually occurs in adults over forty years of age and is the most common form of the disease. Ninety percent of all cases of diabetes are Type II.

These two types of diabetes now affect more than ten million people, or one in every forty Americans. Because diabetes is hereditary, it affects the entire family. With new and improved tests, 600,000 new cases are discovered each year, and the number is steadily increasing.

Because most diabetics lead active lives and are employed, diabetes is not considered the major health problem that it is. Diabetics are twenty-five times more prone to blindness than nondiabetics. Diabetics are twice as prone to strokes and heart disease. Diabetics are five times more prone to gangrene than nondiabetics. (Gangrene often leads to amputation.)

Research efforts continue to find out more about the cause of the disease, its care, and treatment. Many diabetics with eye problems can be helped by a new treatment using lasers. This treatment stops leakage in the retina of the eye and prevents half the vision loss that affects hundreds of thousands of diabetics. Intense laser light can be used to heat and

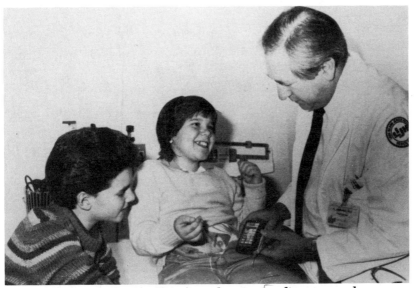

Dr. Cyril Abrams checks Allison's pocket-size insulin pump as her brother Timothy looks on at Long Island Jewish Medical Center. (Newsday.)

seal severely bleeding vessels in the eyes. The new treatment, which can be repeated if necessary, seals the sources of swelling, often preventing further vision loss and, in some cases, improving sight.

Another recent technique used with diabetic children is the insulin pump. The *Journal of Pediatrics*, February 1984, reported the use of this pump with a group of children, aged seventeen months to fifty-three months, who had to be injected with insulin twice daily. The pump is self-injectable and is worn. Results appear to hold promise for future use with this group.

One youngster who is using the pump is Allison Marie Lynch of Mineola, New York. Allison is ten years old and is in the fifth grade at Jackson Avenue School. She is a good student and says reading is her favorite subject. Allison has two sisters and a brother. Her grandfather is the only other diabetic in the family. She has had diabetes for three years. For all of those years, she injected herself with insulin three times a day. Now she wears the pump. Allison is very active and enjoys soccer. Life has changed for her, and she looks forward to dancing. Her attendance at school has been perfect since the pump. The past few years have been difficult, but the future appears hopeful for the Lynches.

ARTHRITIS

A young girl stands and gives her seat to an elderly woman because the enlarged and crooked joints of the woman's right hand prevent her from grasping an overhead strap on the bus.

An old man slowly makes his way across the street. Automobile horns blow sharply as he tries to beat the changing light. His shuffling gait is the result of swollen, painful knees.

A forty-five-year-old man is strapped to the chair beside his bed in a nursing home. All of his limbs are shortened and twisted. He cannot maintain his balance.

All of these people have arthritis—America's most common chronic disease. More than 36 million Americans have some form of arthritis. Because arthritis is not fatal, it does not rank with cancer and heart disease as a major killer. It is, however, responsible for half of all United States worker's compensation claims.

The economic costs of arthritis and musculoskeletal diseases, including medical expenses and lost wages, is estimated to be thirty billion dollars a year. Most people believe that arthritis is a disease of the elderly. This is a myth. Debbie K. is twenty-seven years old and has lived with the disease for twenty-five years.

By the time Debbie was fifteen, she had undergone seven operations on her hips and knees. Despite surgery and various drugs, Debbie attended public school, had many friends, and tried to live as normal a life as possible. At seventeen, she married and had two children. Debbie managed to take care of her family and home. When she was twenty-one, a severe flare-up of the disease left her in a wheelchair. Debbie was referred to the Hospital for Special Surgery in New York. There she received the best and latest of technology. Over a three-year period, Debbie had two total knee replacements, both hips reconstructed, and a triple fusion of an ankle. A wrist realignment and shoulder replacement are scheduled for the future. So far, she has had thirteen operations. Although Debbie sometimes feels like a "Bionic Woman," she is living a fairly normal life with her two healthy children. Without the new technology in surgery and orthopedics, Debbie would be confined to a wheelchair.

The word *arthritis* means joint (arth) and inflammation (itis). There are more than 150 forms of the disease. The type Debbie has is called Juvenile Arthritis. More than 250,000 children are affected with this type of the disease. Most forms of arthritis are chronic, which means that if no cure is found, they may last a lifetime.

For the millions of people who are arthritic, there may be

some relief in the next decade thanks to a horse named Devil's Bag, who was a Champion Two-Year-Old in 1983. Favored to win the 1984 Kentucky Derby, the horse broke two knee bones a week before the race. He was sold shortly after and is now breeding new champion thoroughbred horses, as well as helping to make important progress in arthritis research. His owner, a victim of arthritis, created the Devil's Bag Research Award fund from the horse's earnings of stud fees. Thanks to this horse, special new arthritis research, using the most modern techniques of molecular biology, began recently in five prestigious institutions in the United States. Johns Hopkins, Stanford, Harvard, and Duke universities, and Dartmouth Medical School all received Devil's Bag awards.

Molecular biology, one of the fastest growing fields of modern science, examines the molecules that regulate all body processes at the most basic level. When applied to arthritis, it can open the door to understanding the malfunctions inside certain cells in the body which cause arthritis.

In January 1986 the federal government created a new institute devoted to the study of arthritis and related disorders. The National Institute of Arthritis and Musculoskeletal Diseases will be the first new component of the National Institutes of Health in over a decade. Researchers have impressed officials with findings that have linked arthritis to hormone activity, immune dysfunction, and to genetic factors. The new institute will boost promising areas of arthritis research and ultimately lead to new methods of treatment and prevention.

The institute will also provide funds to pursue other new

developments, such as links between arthritis and abnormalities in the immune system, the role of viruses in triggering arthritis disorders, and new methods of repairing arthritis damage through tissue and bone transplants. Answers seem to come more quickly when a separate institute is set up, says Dr. M. McDuffie, Senior Vice-President, Arthritis Foundation National Office.

FUTURE HOLDS PROMISE

Earlier in this book, the National Institutes of Health was credited as the major support of medical research in the United States. Recently, the new Howard Hughes Medical Institute announced the establishment of twenty-two research institutes in medical schools and hospitals employing 300 scientists in the fields of genetics, immunology, metabolic regulation, and the neurosciences. The institute plans to provide one billion dollars in grants between 1986 and 1990, and the budget will exceed 300 million dollars each year after that. With this additional support, scientists expect major breakthroughs in biomedical research within the next decade.

CHAPTER 7

A Close Look

In 1895, Wilhelm Roentgen, a German physicist, made it possible for doctors to take a closer look. He discovered the X-ray. For his work, Roentgen was awarded the Nobel Prize in 1901. Ever since, researchers and scientists have been trying to look even deeper into the cavities, systems, and operations of the complex functions of the human body.

The X-ray itself has not changed very much over the years. But ways of recording and reporting the findings have changed.

X-RAYS BY TELEPHONE

One system used by many hospitals for reviewing X-rays is called Rapid Telephone Access System (RTAS). This is how it works. A radiologist—a doctor who specializes in the study of X-rays—puts the film on a lighted screen. There is a telephone nearby. He gives a security number and the patient's

Taking an X-ray can be frightening to a small child. A nurse comforts the youngster.

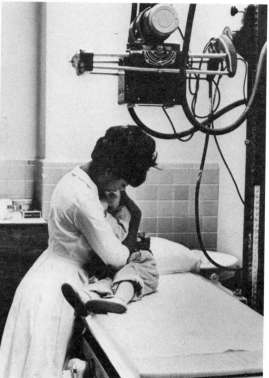

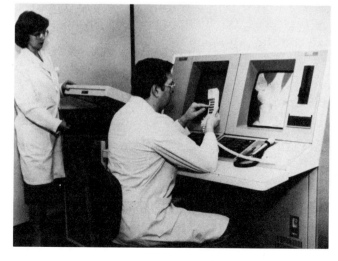

The TEL-X-2400 Teleradiology system permits rapid transmission of diagnostic-quality images over short or long distances, permitting long-distance X-ray diagnosis.

123

I.D. number. Then the doctor dictates the report through the telephone directly into the computer. The computer digitalizes—that is, changes into numbers—the radiologist's voice and stores it on a disc. The moment the doctor finishes talking, the report becomes available. A physician away on vacation or even practicing in another state can dial the computer by using the correct release codes and listen to the recording. This is a type of teleradiology system, which means it uses both the telephone and the X-ray. The chief advantage of the system is the speed with which the report is available for diagnosis, treatment, and consultation.

Another way of communicating what is on an X-ray is used at the University of California Hospital in San Francisco. This computerized system makes it possible to store X-rays in computers and, in less than 30 seconds, to send X-ray pictures across the United States over telephone lines. There is no need to store bulky films. Instead, X-ray information is photographed, converted to digital form, and fed into a computer. The screen provides an excellent image. It is so good that one can't tell the difference between a reconstructed picture and the original film.

According to a news story in *U.S.A. Today,* March 10, 1983, the equipment permits doctors hooked up via telephone lines but thousands of miles apart to examine X-rays and discuss opinions on the system's screens. Traditionally, the way to get an opinion from another doctor was to mail him or her a copy of the film and then wait until it was examined.

Teleradiology will also permit several hookups within one institution. Suppose Dr. K. is in surgery. He is comparing preoperative films with what he has found during the operation. He can call a radiologist, a cardiologist, or anyone else throughout the various departments of the hospital to view the film with him on the system's network.

X-RAYS AND COMPUTERS

"About 1970, a revolutionary event took place. It was the marriage of an X-ray machine with computer-aided nuclear imaging, which resulted in the birth of the CAT scan, as it is popularly known. CAT scan, or computerized axial tomography, is one of the most significant things that has happened in the field of diagnostic medical filming since the invention of the X-ray 75 years earlier. It was the first time that a computer, as part of an instrument, had been used to create a picture of the body," says Dr. Donald L. King, Director of Ultrasound at Columbia Presbyterian Hospital in New York City.

"Tomography is a sectional X-ray. It shows us a sliced image or reflection. The computer cuts down on the radiation and a series of slices gives a more three-dimensional picture," Mr. Farrel, an X-ray technician, says in explaining the complicated machine. "Suppose the doctor saw a tumor on a patient's chest X-ray. He would also see overlaying ribs, blood vessels, arteries, and parts of the heart on top of the tumor. In the tomography, he can isolate the tumor by blocking out all other things. It's like taking a slice of the body, but one slice at a time."

The CAT scan, already in its fifth generation model, continues to give fast and clear pictures. Because of its speed, it is able to record a dynamic scan and even show blood flowing through the heart. Overall, the greatest effect of the CAT scan has been and still is in the evaluation of neurological diseases, brain tumors, and spinal abnormalities. The largest application of the CAT scan is the evaluation of malignant diseases, including their detection, staging, treatment planning, and therapeutic progress.

The evaluation of the traumatized patient is another area where the CAT scan has had a major impact. You may recall that Mrs. Gerney was examined with the scan after assessment in the emergency room. The use of scanners permits many areas of the body to be evaluated rapidly and safely, and, due to its ease of interpretation, the need for exploratory surgery has also been reduced.

Although the CAT scan is one of the most remarkable scientific breakthroughs of our time, it has generated many cost-versus-benefit debates in health-planning agencies. With its million-dollar-plus price tag, the scanner is often judged to be too expensive for many hospitals. However, in Philadelphia, four hospitals within a short distance of each other were able to purchase one CAT scanner between them and share its use. Remote systems and relays made it possible to do this, thus saving over three million dollars. Planned participation enabled the hospitals to share information for consulting and teaching purposes on a twenty-four-hour basis.

A newer scanner will be on the market soon. It has no moving parts, eliminating the X-ray that revolves around the patient in conventional scanners. An electron gun, which is steered and focused by a computer, shoots a beam of electrons at the tungsten rings surrounding the patient. The electrons strike the rings at the speed of light, producing X-ray beams that sweep the patient. It sounds like *Star Wars!*

This twenty-first-century scanner can even make a picture of the amount of blood in heart tissue and can measure blood flow within arteries, the brain, liver, and kidneys. It can allow the doctor to see the knee as the joint is being extended or flexed. It is called a Cine scanner.

X-RAYS, COMPUTERS, AND MAGNETS

Nuclear Magnetic Resonance (NMR) is a scanner that can perform diagnostic functions and more. It can do quantitative analysis or dissection of parts of a tissue sample and provides a means of evaluating the chemical and biological conditions of the tissue sample. The procedure sounds complicated, but follow the explanation slowly. The technique is a sophisticated one that involves putting the patient into a large circular magnet. That magnetic field gets the bearings of a small percentage of the nuclei in the atoms within the patient's body that are in the direction of the magnetic field. It can be used as a diagnostic tool in such cases as the following.

Mr. G. has many symptoms that point toward a possible malignancy. The NMR will identify the type, stage, location, and so on.

Ms. P. recently suffered a stroke. She has some paralysis, speech disorders, and personality changes. Her doctor wants to know if her brain damage can be repaired.

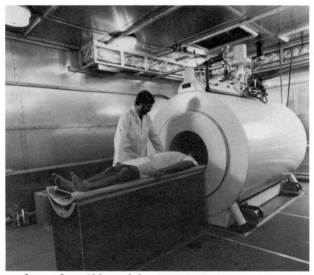

Multi-nuclear (fifteen kiloguass) NMR scanner.

Dorothy W. had epileptic attacks as a young girl. Now as a preteen, the attacks have returned. Her doctor wants to know why. The NMR scanner can look through the patient at any angle and create a three-dimensional reconstruction, using all the storage and processing ability of present-day computers.

Columbia Presbyterian Hospital's advanced scanner is the first clinical system that is powerful enough to look for atoms of hydrogen and phosphorous. "It allows radiologists to study the shape and function of human tissue," says physicist Dr. William Perman. The scanner is the first in the United States. It also contains the most powerful magnet in the world for NMR imaging or reflecting.

NMR will help diagnose cancer. For instance, malignant tumors may contain more hydrogen and phosphorous than normal cells. The computer can check signals from an NMR scan for areas that have more of these two chemicals. This means that doctors could identify individual, extremely small tumors long before these malignancies could be detected with other methods.

X-RAYS, PHYSICS, AND BIOMEDICINE

There is yet another scanner that is used mostly in research at this time. It is called Position Emission Tomography (PET). PET is a new scanner that can be found at Memorial Sloan-Kettering Cancer Center. It is a neat marriage between physics and biomedicine, and gives doctors and scientists a new way of looking at the brain. For the first time, they can see details of brain activity in sickness and in health. They can study how a healthy brain processes information and how mental illnesses such as depression change brain activity.

PET scanning so far is mostly a research activity. There are only about twelve in the United States—two are in New York City. PET scanning is used, at times, for medical treatment. Scientists say it has the potential to revolutionize several branches of medical practice. Using it, they have already discovered some of the early signs of Alzheimer's disease.

X-RAYS AND SOUND WAVES

A revolution in radiology began with the CAT scan. The marriage of a computer with an ultrasound scanner has not been made yet. But it is on the way.

Ultrasound uses the sonar principle, which is a method of detecting and locating objects submerged in water, such as submarines and sunken treasure ships. In medical ultrasound, the instrument sends out a pulse of sound waves and records the echoes as they come back. "This is done very quickly and repeatedly so that we can see a picture much like a TV picture. As you move the scanner over the body, you get a cross-section image of what's inside. It's an auditory picture of organs and clearly heard sounds!" says Dr. King, Director of Ultrasound at Presbyterian Hospital. "We make a cross-sectional picture that changes instantaneously as we move from one spot to another. This is called real time image—one that shows changes as they happen."

Ultrasound and Research

A large area of research that's being studied now is tissue characterization. This means taking returning sound waves and looking at them with the computer for different kinds of information, not just pictures.

Three-dimensional ultrasound scanning will be possible with computers in the future. Doctors will be able to follow and track the position of scanners as they move over the body from one area to another. Three-dimensional scanning up till now has not been possible because of the complexity of the system. The computer must have a large memory capability to keep track of all the information.

"Our diagnostic ability will improve with the use of computers. We will be able to do the kinds of things that were done

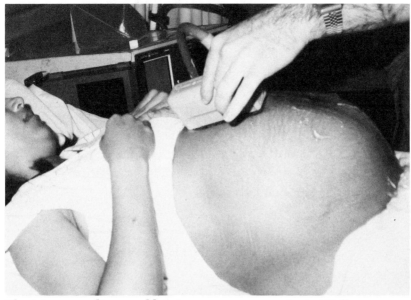

Physician uses ultrasound late in pregnancy on patient at Bellevue. Monitor reveals infant's position and condition.

in the space program where they sent pictures of the moon, Mars, and so on through space and reconstructed them back on earth!" exclaims Dr. King.

Some of the important things about ultrasounds are that it appears harmless, is movable, quite inexpensive, and is able to obtain pictures in real time, or as they are happening. This combination of advantages is not found in any of the other imaging technologies. One final important thing about ultrasound is that it can give some information about tissue, such as whether an object is a fluid or of solid structure.

It is now the most used technique in the clinical practice of medicine, especially in the fields of gynecology and obstetrics. In gynecology, ultrasound is used to investigate infections as well as lesions and tumors in the pelvis. In obstetrics, it is valuable in measuring the growth and age of an unborn baby and is used as a screening procedure to determine certain types of abnormalities in the unborn child.

Is it a boy or a girl? Recent studies show that with a routine ultrasound examination a doctor can safely answer that question up to five months before a baby is born. As early as the fourteenth week of pregnancy, clear pictures are produced that show the unborn baby's sex.

NUCLEAR MEDICINE

Nuclear means cell, but not the kind found in the body. Nuclear medicine is a diagnostic specialty based upon the tracer principle. This is how it works. The patient is injected with a radioactive drug. He or she may feel a slight burning sensation at the injection site, but the procedure itself is painless. The scanner moves back and forth over the site of injection taking images, or pictures. The scanner follows the route of the injected drug through the area under study. Pictures are taken at specific intervals. These pictures can identify diseased tissue. For a clearer picture of the effect upon the area of interest, additional imaging may be performed three or four hours after the injection. The drug poses no danger to the patient and should be eliminated from the body within six hours.

"We can tell if body cells are functioning normally or not," says Dr. Arnold Strashun, assistant professor in Radiology and Internal Medicine at Mount Sinai Medical Center. "By looking into the abnormal biochemistry, we can determine early stages of any disease process."

COMPUTERS TALKING TO COMPUTERS

A new area for growth in radiological technology will be in computer interface, which is when one computer communicates with another computer. Dr. Robin Doris, Medical Director of Radiology at St. James Hospital, Chicago Heights, Illinois, thinks that within three years, a radiologist will be able to sit down at a computer with four screens and on this one unit call up all the ultrasound, CAT scans, and NMR images performed on a patient. The doctor will be able to make correlations and analyses, using this information to confirm final diagnoses. He predicts even greater computerization in the future. Scientists in this field are eagerly awaiting the challenge.

CHAPTER 8

Off and Running

After being left "at the post" for so many years, rehabilitation medicine is off and running. This specialty, which for many years made little advance, has joined others now in using computers and new technology to bring greater fulfillment to the lives of those often overlooked. They are the thirty-six million disabled men, women, and children in the United States who have found a supporter and champion researcher in John Eulenberg and his colleagues at Michigan State University's Artificial Language Laboratory.

SUPER WHEELCHAIRS

Many disabled people use modern wheelchairs, but when compared with the new computerized wheelchair designed by researchers at the Palo Alto Veterans Administration Rehabilitation Research and Development Center, they appear antique.

134

This new wheelchair is the super wheelchair. It works by having sonar sensors flank the wheelchair headrest to pick up the rider's head movements. The sensors then send this information to a small computer on the back of the chair that controls the chair's movement. When the rider nods forward, the chair moves ahead. When he or she nods backward, the chair moves back. When the head is tilted to the right or the left, the chair turns in a circle. If the rider presses a button on the headrest by using the head, the wheelchair stops or starts.

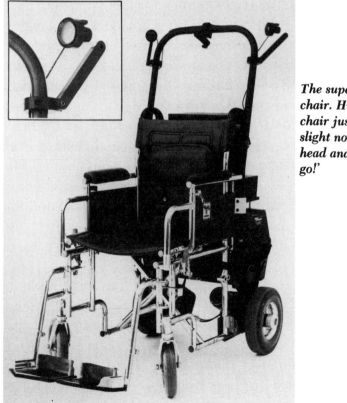

The super wheelchair. Hi-tech chair just needs slight nod of the head and 'Away we go!'

HEARING VOICES

Because of technology, most of the country's seventeen million people with hearing losses can now be helped to hear better through a variety of devices. These range from custom-designed hearing aids to an experimental implant used in cases of nerve deafness. Before computers, deaf people could only call relatives and other deaf people who happened to have the same or compatible telephone equipment.

One innovation allows people who cannot conduct conversations by telephone to use special typewriters and minicomputers that transcribe telephone messages in both directions.

Another revolutionary idea involves middle ear implants. These implants can translate incoming sound vibrations into electric signals that are sent to the brain. In Detroit, Michigan, a twenty-two-year-old student reports that the device did even more than improve her ability to communicate. The implant saved her life. The surgery made it possible for her to hear a siren and so avoid being struck by an oncoming fire truck. Voice recognition machines that allow people to talk to a computer and have their words appear on a screen are available, too.

For the homebound or elderly, there are amplifiers on telephone headsets and lights that flash when the telephone or doorbell rings. There is even a special microphone that allows the deaf to hear the television without having to turn it up too loud. Computers can help deaf children, too. Every effort is being made to have children with disabilities join

136

other children in as many activities as possible. When a class uses computers, this is possible. A deaf child can participate in class, answer the teacher's questions, and joke with other children in the classroom.

ALMOST SECOND SIGHT—THE BLIND

Imagine a talking cash register! The blind cashier merely hits the Braille or regular figures and the total and amount of change to be returned to the customer are spoken loud and clear. How can a blind person identify a ten dollar bill? There's a Paper Money Identifier. Merely slip the bill in the slot face up and a voice tells you the value of the bill! Suppose a blind person feels that a cold is coming on. The temperature can be taken with a computerized thermometer that talks and tells the person if there is a fever. The person merely inserts the thermometer into the mouth and waits a minute or less. When the thermometer is withdrawn, the voice will give the reading.

For the blind student, researcher, or book lover, there is a machine that reads books out loud, another that translates messages into spoken words, and a computer that reads and writes Braille yet doesn't use paper. This reading machine can look at the page and convert the words into speech, allowing the blind to hear the words.

John De Witt is a communications technologist at the American Foundation in New York City. He is one of the country's 1.2 to 1.6 million visually impaired people. Another 500,000 people are legally blind. Mr. De Witt feels the high cost of much of the new technology will be lowered as better production methods are developed. Meanwhile, the foundation's library of 37,000 books, 300-volume rare book collection, and numerous periodicals and research papers are available for reading by the blind and visually impaired.

The foundation's library has a talking computer, which is connected with a national data center in Washington, D.C. This center serves as a "hot line." The computer receives calls which are "talked out" and, at the same time, displayed on its screen. The message can be enlarged up to sixteen times larger than normal print. Mr. De Witt says it helps the blind keep up to date with the announcements of meetings, new legislation concerning the blind, and new books that might interest blind people particularly.

As with sighted children, blind children's schoolwork can improve by using computers. Sashona is a good example. This ten-year-old is blind and has cerebral palsy. She attends a public school in El Cerrito, California. Before she got her computer several years ago, Sashona needed other people to read and write for her. "She learned that if she waited long enough, someone would tell her what to write, and she didn't learn," her mother said. "Now she is going through the process of writing and developing her own thoughts." Sashona is advancing two years for every year spent in school. Her computer has a voice synthesizer and keys that are twice the usual size. She types with her thumbs.

The future looks promising for increases in aids for the handicapped. The U.S. government spends sixty billion dollars annually to support people with disabilities, and up to thirty million dollars goes to researching rehabilitation technology. But almost anyone can develop a new idea. Ms.

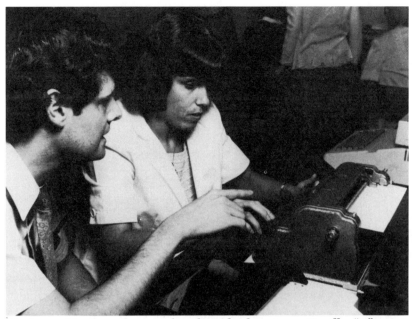

Dr. Larry Gardner shows Deborah Butler how to use Braille, "N" print equipment at Teachers College, Columbia University. (The New York Times.)

Margerine Beaman of Austin, Texas, did just that. She developed the first Braille automatic teller machine, which helps the blind and visually impaired to bank more privately and independently. Some 6000 banks in this country and in several foreign countries now carry Braille instruction sheets detailing the procedures and layout of the keys and slots. Some even have instructions in French and Spanish Braille.

From Boston comes news of a real do-it-yourself invention. Robert Burroughs, a cerebral palsy victim, had difficulty with bank tellers, credit card companies, and stock brokers who wouldn't accept his shaky signature. With the help of biomedical engineers, he designed a handsome ring which when imprinted on documents is his signature. A plastic device holds papers in place while the ring is being pressed down.

"Because the simply designed ring is a familiar piece of jewelry, it does not attract attention," says Mr. Burroughs, who thinks other physically handicapped people can benefit from having a ring of their own. "Receiving a patent was wonderful. But an even greater thrill was American Express's recognition and approval," he says.

MADE TO ORDER

When Ms. Cross needs a knee joint, Mr. Pines a hip joint, and Ms. Lathrop an elbow joint, they are custom-made using the same technology that designed jet engines, skyscrapers, and modern furniture. The new joints are ready for implantation in two weeks.

All of this takes place at the Hospital for Special Surgery in New York City. Surgeons and bioengineers start with a reference bank of implant designs, special software, and a terminal on which modifications can be made. The design of one joint is changed according to a specific patient's need by comparing the design shown on the screen to X-rays and cross sections of the patient's bone. The staff reviews the drawings, which can be produced in less than one minute. The next step is to punch the design into the computer. This then produces a tape that can be fed into various machines that cut the implant from materials such as stainless steel, polyethylene, and chromium cobalt alloy. Dr. Albert H. Berstein explains, "It's similar to going into a Buick dealer and wanting an automobile. The dealer has a list of specifications you can choose from, and after you've chosen, you will have a Buick like no one else's."

Soon the system will allow surgeons to choose or design a prosthesis, or artificial limb, by responding to simple questions. At present, the cost seems high. It is about five thousand dollars for a knee. In the future, the hospital's system, with some modifications, will drive the cost down.

BODY BUILDERS

For the sports enthusiast, there is an exercise machine called Cybex II. Young people like Tyrone use it to strengthen their muscles after they have been injured. Tyrone is a basketball player and is anxious to get back to his team. The machine sets the speed of muscle contraction, and the resistance that the machine gives matches Tyrone's. Michael Kroll, a research physical therapist at the Hospital for Special Surgery, says that this is a safe way to exercise because the machine does not go beyond Tyrone's physical limits. Besides exercises, the Cybex II is used to measure the strength of major body joints and muscles so that appropriate programs of rehabilitation can be planned for individual patients.

Penny Kroll, Michael's wife, is a physical therapist, too. She works at the Hospital for Joint Diseases, fifty blocks to the south of her husband's laboratory. Computers are used here, too. In addition to patients, many tennis players, joggers, ballet dancers, and marathon runners can be found

Tyrone uses the Cybex at hospital for special surgery as therapist supervises.

in the gymnasium, using various pieces of equipment. Ms. Kroll says that using appropriate muscles for a typical function is important. Using the computer, muscle activity is measured so that exercise can be more effective. The computer's measurements are correct and instant. Fencers and dancers also use computers in gait analysis and testing. They want to know what muscles they're using, when they're using them, and how they're using them. Ms. Kroll helps them with personal training that improves their performance.

There is a treadmill here with a built-in computer that assures accuracy of speed and grade. It is used by patients with disabilities involving their lower legs, particularly shin areas. Therapists can prescribe a corrective program after they review computer tapes of the patients' performances.

SPORTS MEDICINE

What do Mary Lou Retton, the Refrigerator, Larry Bird, Chris Evert-Lloyd, and John McEnroe have in common? They are all professional athletes who want to perform in top condition all of the time. Sports medicine helps them do this. Doctors in this growing specialty use computers to study the cause of injuries so athletes can compete with a full understanding of how to use their bodies in ways that limit injuries.

How do you measure performance? The average lay person looks for skill, balance, speed, smoothness, and accuracy. But the athlete's measurement of performance is much more complex. By using computers, what really happens in a performance is available for immediate review. Knowledge of strength or deficiency when making comparisons of limbs is very important and may determine whether or not an athlete succeeds.

Biomechanics sports—a new subdivision within sports medicine—analyzes human motion. Phil Rosenthal, assistant director, Institute of Sports Medicine at Lenox Hill Hospital, New York, says the professionals are studying how the length or strength of a limb affects motion. Other questions concern the relationship of position and speed. For instance, a film of an athlete performing in his or her sport can be analyzed and

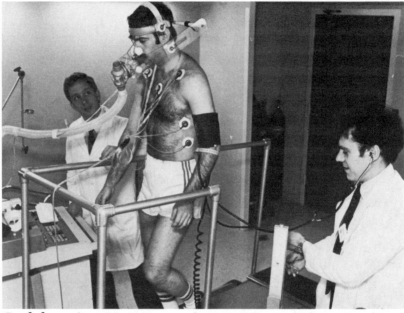

Graded exercise stress test measuring oxygen consumption as a major index of fitness at the Institute of Sports Medicine at Lenox Hill Hospital, New York.

with the aid of a computer, plotted at certain points to determine what makes an outstanding performance. Is it the angle of the arm? The elevation of the shoulders in the backstroke? The push-off when vaulting from the floor horse? Does the kind of tennis racquet or vaulter's pole make the difference? The researchers are trying to help the athletes to perform at the peak of their ability without sustaining injuries.

Computers are influencing the design of braces, track shoes, and even swimsuits. Football equipment undergoes regular change. The ability to simulate the actions of an athlete in motion may contribute to our understanding of the mechanics of human motion. This is important too in the area of equipment design. What kinds of material can best protect a knee, a head, or a shoulder? Along with speed, there is the concern for safety.

For the past few years, the country has been on a fitness kick—with aerobics exercise programs from movie stars, marathons, an increased awareness of good nutrition, and so on. What helps the athlete will eventually help the general public. Mr. Rosenthal believes that in the near future, a person will arrive at a physical fitness center with a list of his or her prerequisites, which will be typed into a computer. The computer will issue a prescription of therapeutic exercises based on the individual's need.

DESIGNERS OF TREATMENT PROGRAMS

Dr. John Gianutsos is one rehabilitation specialist who is totally involved with technology. He designs and creates individual programs for patients at New York University's Institute of Rehabilitation Medicine. Lynne T. is one of his patients. Sixteen months ago, Lynne suffered a stroke that affected her right upper and lower extremities. Lynne suffered some memory loss and speech impairment as well. After completing regular physical and occupational therapies, she was ready for intensive treatment of her right upper extremity. Her right hand was functionally limited. The staff worked on helping Lynne to extend her fingers. For most

Lynne uses biofeedback with one of Dr. John Gianusos' custom designed programs for restoring strength to hands and arms. Therapist Beverly guides her.

stroke victims, the clutched fist is the most difficult disability to overcome.

Dr. Gianutsos designed a training program using electrodes that are placed on Lynne's arm and hand. As she tries to straighten her fingers, she looks at a video monitor that shows her progress. Lynne had to work hard to reach a preset goal of the extension of her fingers, which required extra muscle power. Whenever she reached her goal, electrical stimulation helped her to open her hand. Gradually, stimulation was decreased, and Lynne performed without it. As soon as she was able to open her hand voluntarily upon command, Dr. Gianutsos helped her progress to writing.

There are many other items in the laboratory that are the product of Dr. Gianutsos's dynamic, creative intelligence. One is a weight shift training program that helps a disabled person learn how to control balance. Another is a wheelchair control program that trains people how to control their chairs. These patients use standard chairs, which are usually operated with the use of one hand.

Dr. Gianutsos also designs video games for young children. He began with toy cars, using remote control devices to stimulate muscle activity. The doctor noticed that youngsters spent a lot of time with the toys. Now he has video games, such as Breakout, where the action is controlled by the child. There are several versions of the game, which record activity in one muscle or two muscles that work alternately.

Another professional who designs individual patient programs is Dr. Robert Volin, a speech pathologist at the Manhattan Veterans Administration Hospital. His work is with aphasia patients—those with limited or no ability to communicate. In his laboratory, a stroke victim sits in front of the computer using a program designed to improve his ability to form correct sentences. The program uses simple sentences that are structured to follow a basic format. The sentences are scrambled. An example might be DOWN ON SIT YOUR CHAIR. The patient stares at the scrambled sentence. When he or she figures out the correct sequence, the patient types the first letter of each word in the properly ordered sentence. When the right letter is hit, the entire word is printed out on the screen, and in the proper position. The patient then advances to the next word, until the sentence is completed. The patient is given an enforcer, which is a kind of reward. The reward can be as simple as the word "good" printed on the screen or it can be more complicated.

Dr. Volin feels that one of the nicest things about patients working with computers is that the machines don't make judgments about them. Sometimes when patients work closely with a therapist, they tend to feel humiliated and uncomfortable when a mistake is made. This happens despite the understanding and compassion shown by the therapist. Patients feel stupid because they cannot do things that were formerly routine—such as talking, chewing, whistling, or grasping. The computer is neither threatening nor condemnatory. So the patient who may become impatient even with the most supportive doctor will sit alone with the computer for hours and work conscientiously to regain lost skills.

There are other common, disabling conditions that can be helped with computers. One is epilepsy, which is probably one of the oldest and least understood conditions. In the United States, hundreds of thousands of children and adults are afflicted with this disability. Help for these people appears to be within the realm of possibility because of an innovative research study using self-management and self-control of bodily functions. This is called biofeedback. The therapy is done at the International Center for the Disabled (ICD) in New York City.

According to Robert Fried, Ph.D., director of the institute, eighteen epileptic clients are currently taking part in the study, which initially began in February 1982. All except one have shown considerable improvement in their conditions since coming to the center. Of the seventeen showing improvement, five have not suffered a grand mal seizure (loss

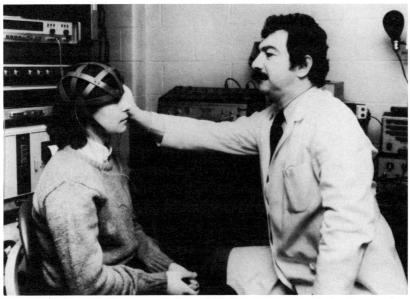

Dr. Robert Fried, director of the Rehabilitation Research Institute using biofeedback in treatment.

of consciousness followed by violent convulsions) in several months. Some have even been able to stop seizures when they felt them coming on.

Through the use of the center's specially designed equipment, the clients learn to control breathing functions and, in particular, to limit the amount of carbon dioxide they exhale. In this way, they control blood flow to the brain, which, in turn, affects brain function and increases the amount of oxygen the brain receives. This stops the seizure or at least reduces its severity.

This seizure control research study is the only one of its kind in the United States. Its success has encouraged the institute to seek other areas where the use of the clients'

149

biofeedback and self-management may be used to help them become independent and employable.

A GIANT STEP

Although new technology and research have led to more successful treatment programs for the disabled, there is still the difficulty in finding employment for them. One project that is helping to solve this problem is Project MATCH, based at Long Island University in New York. By 1995, it is projected that such programs, will be duplicated on campuses across the United States. The project's objective is to train handicapped people to use computers and then get them out into the work place. The project director helps employers who are seeking qualified computer-trained people. Because of computerization of the work place, new worlds and jobs have opened up to the disabled.

In the not-too-distant future, voice synthesizers that read to the blind from computers, oversized keyboards, keyboards operable without the use of hands, sonar devices, and computerized telephone communication will make the work place accessible to people with a range of disabilities.

Then, when the work is done, there is Achilles—an affiliate of the New York Road Runners Club. Achilles has seventy-five members and is growing. Members, aged six to sixty-seven, meet weekly at the International Running Center to get information about races and work out in Central Park. For Tom C., twenty-three years old and blind, running has helped him gain self-confidence and courage. "It gives people

Children, alumni of pediatric orthopedic surgery, enjoy the normal functioning of their feet playing soccer. They were treated for crippling club foot.

the chance to see that they are not alone and that people care," he says. Some of the long-distance runners live as far away as Australia, and are trained by mail.

In a recent New York City marathon, thirteen members of Achilles not only competed but finished the entire twenty-six miles. Seeing the disabled runners helps other runners, too. They work a little harder and realize that running is a universal sport.

CHAPTER 9

The Supporting Cast

In any major production, there are the behind-the-scenes people who work very hard supporting the team effort. They make it possible for the stars to perform like stars. The stars in this case may be prized scientific equipment or the hands and mind of a highly skilled practitioner. Without the support of many allied services, health scientists would not be able to perform their miracles, much less their day-to-day routines. One of these supports is an information system that permits communication between the stars, the institution, and the rest of the cast.

FOR THE RECORD

All institutions share one basic problem: how to store vast amounts of information so that selected pieces can be made available and linked to other pieces quickly and efficiently.

Across the country, most hospitals depend upon an almost totally manual system of handling records. Just imagine the pieces of paper involved in even one patient's admission to the hospital.

Joseph K. was admitted to the hospital because of injuries received in an automobile accident. He suffered fractured legs, cracked ribs, bruises, and a concussion. During the first day, Mr. K. had many laboratory tests, X-rays, and examinations by doctors who represented three services—orthopedics, surgery, and neurology. The next day, he saw the dietician, social worker, physical therapist, respiratory therapist, and a clerk from the billing office. By the third day, operation and anesthesia records, consultation forms, drug orders, and X-ray reports had joined the almost-packed patient's chart. Each time he left his room for a test, the chart accompanied him and more paper was added. After a week, there were more than fifty pieces of paper jammed between the metal covers. When Mr. K. was discharged, the papers were clipped together and sent to medical records storage. With handling and stacking, will the records remain intact?

An almost paperless hospital is New York University Medical Center, a large teaching institution in New York City. It is probably one of the best examples of a fully computerized (95 percent) system.

Martina Eng, a staff nurse there on a surgical unit, picks up a patient care worksheet when she reports for the afternoon shift. The worksheet has been generated by the computer within the last hour and is up to date on patients' current orders, diagnoses, nursing procedures, diets, activities, and the laboratory work done, collected, or waiting for reports.

Mitchell McDaniel, Director of Medical Records at Mt. Sinai Hospital in New York City, operating storage and retrieval apparatus.

This printout has replaced the traditional Cardex (patient information card) for each patient that was usually found at the nurses' station. The worksheet will be referred to frequently during the next eight hours as Ms. Eng cares for her patients. She'll make notes on the worksheet and use it as a basis for a report to the nurse on the following shift and then discard it. The night nurse will receive a similar worksheet issued by the printer. This one, generated within the last hour of Ms. Eng's shift, will contain the latest information on the patients. Each nursing unit in the hospital has four terminals and one printer. Any procedure ordered for pa-

154

tients must be done through the system, since there are no paper order sheets or charts.

"This is the Technician Data Systems—a level 3 system," explains Ms. Patsy Marr, Director of Hospital Information Services (HIS) at the hospital. "The system is fully integrated and designed for direct professional face-to-face interaction." The director reveals that the hospital initiated computerization between 1979 and 1980 by altering Technicon's software programs to meet the hospital's needs. The nursing staff was the first group to be trained in the operation of the system. There are 730 in-patients on the system and 34 different departments that interact directly with the system. An average of 4300 staff people use the system. The Medical Center personnel have their own unique codes and work with the system as necessary.

"As a new employee," Ms. Eng remembers, "I attended classes one hour a day for six weeks. Part of my instructions were programmed—a self-learning package which was rather routine and used to imitate 'real life' situations. Most of us learned it in five weeks." During the peak training periods, like July 1st when residents are rotated, a staff of twenty-three people are involved in training. At other times, about eleven staff members maintain the system by changing screens, adding or removing drugs, adding tests and new activities for various users.

"I loved it from the very beginning. We were able to eliminate most of the routine charting and could spend more time comforting patients. Some nurses were not too sure that it helped. They thought computers meant more work, at first." Ms. Eng reports.

Ms. Eng thinks the most useful thing about the system for nurses is data retrieval. Laboratory reports are available almost immediately, medications to be given and any reasons for not giving them appear on the screen. For instance, a patient may have refused the medication or been off the floor having a test when the medication was due. When doctors write orders, they are automatically entered into the terminal and the printer. To select information a "light pen" is used. By touching the video screen, "pages" of information arranged in a logical series appear.

Nurse Martina Eng uses light pen at "paperless" University Hospital, New York City.

A physician can walk up to any terminal, enter his or her special authorization code, and immediately a list of his or her patients appears. The doctor may then select a patient by touching that person's name with the light pen. All essential information about that individual becomes available on the screen. Should the doctor decide to enter an order, such as a Gastro-Intestinal examination (G.I. series), he or she selects the X-ray, ordering it directly with a touch of his pen. The order is transmitted to the radiology department (X-ray) and the terminal at the nurses' station on the floor where the patient is located. This happens because orders that involve several departments have been integrated into the system, so they are automatically dispersed to each of these departments at the same time. In addition to nursing areas, terminals are located in more than twenty other departments, including EKG, pharmacy, dietary, social service, medical records, and cardiac catherization.

Despite computerization, there are some procedures that are still performed manually. These include the writing of nurses' progress notes, doctors' initial histories and physical assessment, and doctors' progress notes. These areas require free-flowing narrative writing. To enter such detail would require all doctors and nurses to be skilled in typing, and they are not. But the discharge summary, which is a duplicate of the manual one, is done through the system.

Aside from planned and unplanned computer "rest periods," the system functions efficiently 95 percent of the time.

One other system of interest is being installed by the network of Veterans Administration Hospitals. Soon every veterans' hospital in the United States will be linked by

157

computers. The new system will permit a New York vet to be treated in California and a vet on vacation in Florida to be helped there—vets may request medical care from any of the hospital centers in the country. The computer will permit easy access to data for purposes of research, too.

ELECTROCARDIOGRAPH

The electrocardiograph (EKG) is an instrument for recording the changes in a heartbeat. The graph so produced which shows the activity (beats, rhythm, pace) of the heart is called an electrocardiogram. Minerva Rivera, registered cardiology technician, is the supervisor of the EKG Department at Mount Sinai Hospital, New York.

The hospital uses the very latest in equipment. In the department is a simulator. By using this device, it is possible to imitate, or simulate, activity similar to that in a patient's heart. Each machine is checked by the simulator for tachycardia (fast heartbeat), bradycardia (slow heartbeat), or heart block before it leaves the department. "It's important to have everything in good working order. It saves time. Also, watching the technician look for errors in readings can cause anxiety in patients."

As she checks out a machine, the supervisor uses a fictitious name, age, I.D., and bed location. When the copy emerges, all of these data are at hand plus readings from the twelve leads placed on the "body." Ms. Rivera explains, "This is what happens at the bedside. And meanwhile, the same information is fed to the main computer here in the department. Data are analyzed and a hard copy issued from the printer. The system is foolproof. Three copies are available, allowing us to check and match copies from the EKG machine with those issued by the main computer. These copies are stored. But, at any given moment, they can be retrieved." Ms. Rivera cites an example: "All EKGs taken in the Emergency Room are fed directly into the computer. If Mr. Philip D. visits the Emergency Room because of chest pain, the technician merely asks the computer if there are any EKGs in his name in the computer. If the response is positive, the technician requests them. The main computer will issue the

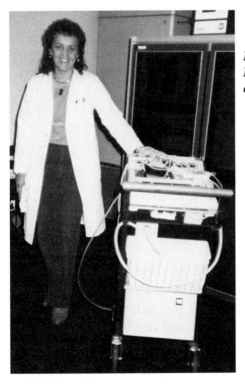

Minerva Rivera, supervisor of Mount Sinai's Electro-cardiography Department.

printouts, which are promptly sent to the Emergency Room by messenger."

The system has been operating since 1981, and all the technicians are comfortable with it. "For them, it has created motivation and a desire to learn more about the new technology," Ms. Rivera says.

MR. FIXITS

Behind every perfectly operating piece of machinery is a good biomechanical technologist who tests, repairs, and maintains the equipment in the best possible condition. Usually located far away from the heart of the hospital, these technicians spend their days and nights making sure that all of the expensive machinery is in good working condition. Surgeons could not operate, radiologists could not give treatments, and nurses could not monitor patients' conditions without these skilled assistants.

At Parkland Memorial Hospital in Dallas, Texas, Bob Johnson and Michael Calderone are two of the six men who work in the Bio-Engineering Department, supervised by Jim Wallace. The very large, brightly lit room is filled with equipment. Some of it is new, but most pieces are in various stages of repair. Besides various monitors, there are respirators, pumps, EKG machines, automated sphygmomanometers (blood pressure taking devices), and numerous other not so easily recognizable items. Michael is repairing a fetal monitor while Bob checks out a new intravenous pump. Both men basically have been trained on the job, although Bob

Checking out fetal monitors—
Michael Calderone at
Parkland Memorial Hospital,
Dallas, Texas.

plans to attend a community college and earn an Associates'
Degree in Biomedical Technology. Bob knows that as the use
of technological aids increases, the need for trained technologists will keep pace.

In some institutions, there are dedicated professionals who
can design or transform a surgeon's wish into a reality. Heinz
Rosskothen is one such technologist. He has directed instru-
mentation for Ophthalmology at Columbia Presbyterian Hospital in New York City for nineteen years. "I make things that
have never existed before," says the master instrument
maker. "When a clinician or scientist needs something that is
unavailable commercially, they come in, explain what they
want, and I make it." He holds many patents for his efforts.

This craftsman works with almost every kind of material, such as plexi-glass, aluminum, teflon, and stainless steel. When necessary, he becomes a "doctor on call" for repairs. "Although this is not really my area, I'm sometimes called to the operating room to fix a piece of equipment. I just go in there and within five minutes, it's fixed." Otherwise, a surgeon may have to wait hours for a repairman. Thirty-two years ago, Mr. Rosskothen began his career as an apprentice in the tool and die industry in Germany. He enjoys his work, and knowing that one of his designs is helping patients who were totally blind to see makes his work even more satisfying.

THE PHARMACISTS

Almost all pharmacy software modules include an intravenous (I.V.) program and a unit dose program. A feature of the I.V. program is label-making. Orders are entered into the computer through the keyboard, and as soon as the entry is completed, the necessary I.V. labels are made by the printer. At the Pharmaceutical Service of Hutzel Hospital in Detroit, Michigan, the "I.V. day" runs twenty-four hours, from noon through noon of the following day. When a new order is entered into the system, sufficient labels are printed to last throughout the I.V. day. An I.V. order remains active in the computer system until a command is given to discontinue it or until a programmed stop date is reached, when the computer automatically discontinues the order.

Other features of this program include charging and crediting patient accounts. At Hutzel, a patient is not charged for an I.V. medication until it is actually scheduled for administration. This approach to charging saves time needed to credit doses that are not administered. Only one hard copy report is issued. This is the Notice of Drug Expiration report, which notifies the pharmacy of drug stop dates.

The unit dose program is supported by two computers and a printer. Orders are entered into the computer, and the necessary labels are printed. The computer is also used to print free-form labels for drugs that are prepackaged. Like the I.V. mixtures, the computer automatically charges for unit dose medication actually dispensed. Again, patients are not charged for a medication until the scheduled administration time. For example, Mr. T. is to get Thyroid extract Gr. 2 every morning for ten mornings. He will be charged each day after 10:00 A.M. rather than for ten doses at the beginning or end of the period.

Hutzel uses a medication profile system, too. Each time a new medication order is entered into the computer, that order becomes part of the patient's profile. Pharmacist William Cornelis explains: "Our procedure is that every order is compared with the patient's computerized profile. We check for medication duplication or therapeutic incompatibilities. The computer profile is very complete, and it can be tailored to recall specific information. The profile can be brought up on the monitor to review discontinued active drug orders, schedule PRN orders (orders to take the drug when necessary or needed), I.V. unit dose orders, or all orders."

When pharmacists talk about the future of their profession, they use the term "prosumer." The term refers to the consumer who produces what he needs for himself. For example,

All Pharmacy Departments of PATHMARK Chain will soon use computers to process customers' prescriptions. Before filling a prescription, the pharmacist will punch up the customer's profile to see if there are possible dangerous interactions between the new drug and other facets of his or her life. A customer's profile contains vital statistics plus diagnoses, drug and food allergies, chronic illnesses and drugs commonly taken and physicians' names and addresses.

individuals take their own blood pressure, test urine for pregnancy, and perform throat cultures and Pap smears. Kenneth Barker, Ph.D., head of the Department of Pharmacy, Auburn University School of Pharmacy, Auburn, Alabama, thinks that future hospital outpatient pharmacies may look like chain pharmacies. The consumer will be in control, and the pharmacies will try to give them whatever they want and can pay for. Consumers will want to know more about their medications, too. So pharmacists will talk with clients from counseling booths set up in stores and pharmacies.

Telematic will be in use through a Videodisk PPI (patient package insert), a low-cost video disc the size of a quarter or smaller that would be sold for fifty cents with, or separately from, any drug. The disc would explain in sound and visual image how the drug is expected to work, its possible side effects, and how to control these side effects. The patient would play the disc while the pharmacist wrapped his drugs.

Another potential device is the "pill machine" envisioned by Dr. Barker. "It should only be a matter of time before the dispensing of routine medication is completely automated, leaving maintenance of the machines as the only task requiring human intervention. Unfortunately, the potential impact of this on patient care has, so far at least, received little attention."

These are only a few of the supporting cast. There are also the maintenance, security, dietary, sterile supplies, and laundry departments among the many others that support the stars in their sterling performances.

CHAPTER 10

Photo Finish—A Look to the Future

There are so many new and exciting developments in the health sciences that only a few could be covered in detail in this book. The pictures in this chapter will give the reader a peek at some of the amazing triumphs of the technological revolution that will influence health sciences in the twenty-first century. None of these developments would be possible without the people behind them.

One of the future scientists is Dr. Joseph Haddad, a third-year resident at Columbia Presbyterian Hospital. "What a time to be in medicine! The next decade will be exciting and challenging," he says. "I will be practicing in an era of such things as plastic blood vessels, artificial red blood cells, and pacemakers that slow down the heartbeat." A wrist alarm for diabetics that can detect low blood sugar levels even during sleep and alert the wearer in time to take proper action will join the automatic insulin pump. These will make taking injections out of date. "I can envision a doctor really getting to know his patients, because he'll have the time. With the use of the *Smart Card Health Record* and its microchip of 50,000 pieces of information, a patient's entire medical history is available instantly. This credit-card-sized device will be carried in one's wallet."

Dr. Haddad looks forward to sensors that can measure internal substances, such as blood chemistry, without entering the body; gene probes and man-made antibodies that cure and treat diseased tissues; and noninvasive techniques that make it possible to diagnose without surgery.

The young doctor continues with enthusiasm. "The gene therapy which may be the answer to some hereditary diseases like hemophilia and cystic fibrosis is well on its way. The therapy will be similar to bone marrow transplantation. Instead of bone, we will use the patient's own cells!"

The work being done in cancer therapy now is very promising. "I find the whole idea of the cancer-fighting 'magic bullet' to be fantastic!" Within the next ten to fifteen years, the drug antibody idea will be a fact. Like guided missiles, drug antibodies will single out and kill individual cancer cells.

Other scientists share the feelings of young Dr. Haddad and are worried about the source of our future medical explorers. Unlike Japan, Russia, and Germany where required science and mathematics courses begin in the first grade, the United States depends upon a small group of very talented people to carry out research. Up to 90 percent of foreign high school graduates are proficient or well trained in

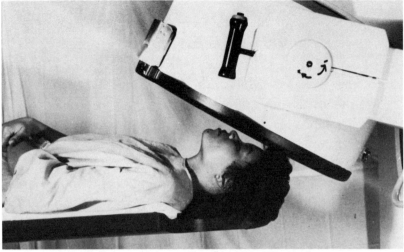

Nuclear medicine in treatment at Presbyterian Hospital.

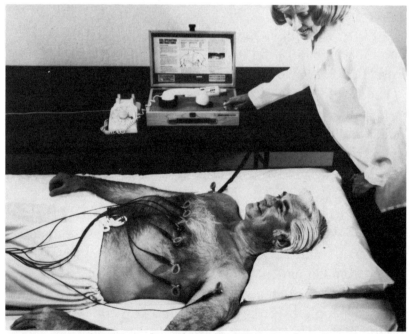

A computerized EKG machine that takes EKG signals and sends them through the telephone lines to a remote computer for immediate processing.

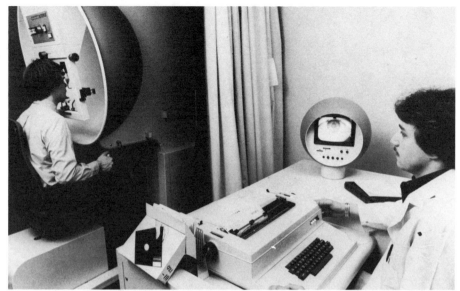

A technician at Wills Eye Hospital in Philadelphia, PA, uses the Octopus Visual Field Tester—the standard in measuring changes in visual fields from glaucoma damage.

Louis Schwartz, M.D., readies Wills' new Yag laser for use. The Yag is the most powerful and precise laser yet.

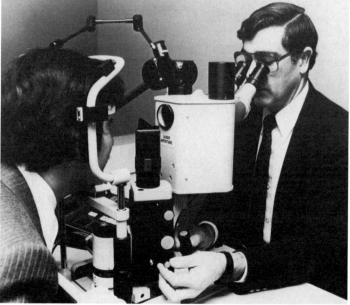

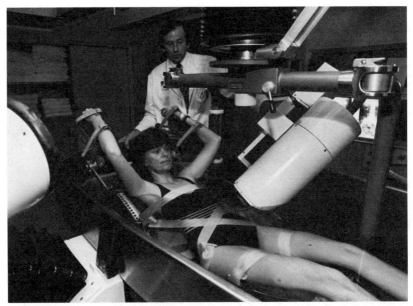

Dr. Robert Riehle of New York Hospital with patient in the kidney stone crusher machine, "Lithotriper." Stones are crushed by shock waves or sonic boom.

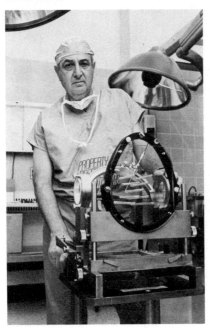

Dr. Edgar Houseplan of Presbyterian Hospital, N.Y. City with new equipment to diagnose and treat brain tumors.

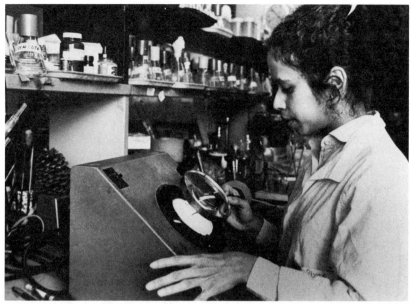

Janet Charles, a Hunter student, studying bacterial transformation in a course on molecular genetics.

mathematics and science, but just 6 percent of U.S. graduates reach a comparable level of ability.

According to a recent study completed at the University of Northern Illinois, an estimated 90 percent of American high school graduates will not be able to perform routine tasks in tomorrow's high tech world. For this reason, President Reagan has established the Young Astronaut program to attract young people into the study of space-related sciences. The goal of the program is not to train future astronauts or to transform them into scientists but to prepare them for the technological challenge ahead.

Young Astronaut chapters are being organized all around the country. Led by teachers or community leaders, young people are studying math, engineering, physics, computers, and other space-related subjects. The tragic deaths of the astronauts on the *Challenger* launched in January 1986 has increased rather than diminished the interest in space. The next teacher-astronaut has been selected, and there are demands for the teaching of science courses earlier in elementary school and for the application of strict science requirements in high school.

Some cities, such as New York, are offering other kinds of programs. Minority Access to Research Careers (MARC) is a

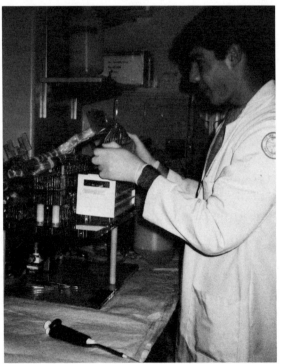

Dalton Conley at work with Cell Harvester, which collects cells onto filter paper, at Rockefeller University where he completed his research.

program operating at Hunter College of the City University of New York. The program is designed to encourage qualified undergraduate minority students to enter careers in the biomedical sciences by offering research participation in one of seventeen laboratories. Students enroll in a variety of science courses, work under the supervision of faculty members on research projects, and prepare written reports. Students receive annual scholarships and reimbursement of tuition and fees. The program is funded by the National Institutes of Health.

Another way to get involved and develop scientific interests and skills is to join the Junior Academy, a division of The New York Academy of Sciences. There are academies in other cities, but New York has the only student-governed academy. Membership is open to all high school students, who are offered a variety of activities. Each member receives a subscription to *The Sciences* (an Academy publication), and monthly lectures, instruction in computers, field trips, and tutorials if needed. The membership fee is five dollars a year. Every April, the Junior Academy holds a Science Fair where students can compete for prizes. During the year, members work on projects in university labs around the city and in this way receive mentorship and exposure to important research. Students are encouraged to become a part of scientific teams and to present research papers.

Two Stuyvesant High School seniors who are members of the Academy were semi-finalists in the National Westinghouse Science Talent Search. Dalton Conley is one of them. He has been working on his project at the Payne Whitney Clinic of New York Hospital and Rockefeller University. The

Rena Moy using the Microtome to make sections of bat brain tissue which will be viewed under the microscope in a study of parasitic infection in bats.

project's title is "Lymphoblast Transformation and Cyclic AMP Levels in Intact Human Lymphocytes"—a very impressive title and subject! Dalton is studying the effect of stress on immune response. Patients undergoing stress and depression are subjects in the study.

Rena Moy is the same age as Dalton. She finds time for tennis, gymnastics, and dance, despite her involvement with an interesting project at Cornell University Medical College. The project is "The Periodicity Account of the New Species Litomosa Wimsatti Microfilariae in the Bat Molossus ater." Rena came upon her study accidentally. Bats were imported from Trinidad for use in a reproductive study, but they had a high death rate. Rena is seeking the cause of death in these bats. Some questions have been answered but others remain unanswered.

Both young people will continue their scientific interests in college and into their adult life. They will join others like them to create a society of miracle workers for the twenty-first century.

ABOUT THE AUTHOR

ESSIE E. LEE, a professor of Community Health Education at Hunter College, New York, has a background in health, guidance, and education. Dr. Lee, a graduate of Columbia University, has devoted many years to research, prevention, and intervention techniques and strategies in the field of drug addiction. A former nurse, counselor, and teacher, she finds that these occupations have helped to formulate concepts for the practice of preventive medicine, another one of her interests. Dr. Lee serves on several boards, foundations, and health service organizations. Her leisure activities include sports fishing, travel, and collecting Asian artifacts. Dr. Lee writes about a variety of topics, including health careers, alcohol, women, marriage and families, and teenage depression.

Index